THE RAINBOW'S END

'Why should God choose to speak to Mr Noah about important matters like building an ark and saving the animals?' said Mrs Noah as she bundled up their clothes. 'He's a good man, but he's not all that special. His carpentry's a nightmare and as for the animals…! He runs a mile at the sight of a spider!'

Mrs Noah's doubts are just the first of Mr Noah's problems. The tortoises are in danger of missing the boat, the camels have got the hump and then the animals threaten to revolt. Worst of all, the water is still rising when the ark becomes wedged between some rocks!

AVRIL ROWLANDS is the author of many books for children. For Lion Publishing these include *Tales from the Ark, More Tales from the Ark* and *The Animals' Christmas*. Among Avril's hobbies are swimming, walking, theatre and steam railways.

As always, I am indebted to my dear friend,
Leslie Guest, for his love, encouragement and support.
Also my warmest thanks to Claire Nelson and
Paul Greenwood for their help and enthusiasm.

The Rainbow's End

& Other Tales from the Ark

Avril Rowlands
Illustrations by Rosslyn Moran

LION
Children's Books

Published by
Lion Publishing plc
Sandy Lane West, Oxford, England
www.lion-publishing.co.uk
ISBN 0 7459 4073 0

First edition 1999
10 9 8 7 6 5 4 3 2 1 0

A catalogue record for this book is available
from the British Library

Typeset in 11.5/15 Zapf Calligraphic BT
Printed and bound in Great Britain
by Cox & Wyman Ltd, Reading

CONTENTS

1
NOAH'S TALE

Mr Noah was having a bad dream. He lay tossing and turning in bed, waking his wife by his restlessness. She prodded him once or twice, but Mr Noah only tossed and turned even more. At last he flung out his arms, hit Mrs Noah squarely on the nose, and sat bolt upright in bed.

'No God!' he shouted. 'Not me! Choose someone else! I don't like animals!'

'Whatever is the matter?' asked his wife.

Mr Noah shook his head. 'I've been having a terrible dream.'

'Must have been the onions you ate last night,' said Mrs Noah, climbing out of bed in order to pick up the bedclothes that had slipped to the floor. 'They kept repeating on me, too.'

Then Mr Noah climbed out of bed and began to pace up and down. 'I dreamt that the world would be destroyed as it had become so wicked.'

'I told you not to eat so many,' said his wife calmly, tucking in the sheets.

'It would rain for forty days and forty nights until the whole earth was flooded...'

'Or perhaps it was the wine...' Mrs Noah climbed back into bed and pulled the bedclothes up around her ears. 'I said you shouldn't drink so much. Now do come back to bed. We've a busy day tomorrow.'

'But you and I and our three sons and their wives would be saved, as well as two of every animal, insect and bird...'

'I never heard anything so ridiculous,' said Mrs Noah, and she turned over and went to sleep.

But Mr Noah could not sleep, so he climbed out of bed and tiptoed out of the house.

His farm lay silent and peaceful under an inky black sky. The stars were shining and moonlight drenched his vineyard with a silver light. Mr Noah touched a bunch of grapes. They were round and fat and still warm from the sun. It would be a good harvest. A splendid harvest.

Perhaps, he thought, his dream *had* been caused by eating too many onions or drinking too much wine at dinner. The world being destroyed? What nonsense! Only his family surviving? What rubbish! Feeling a good deal calmer, Mr Noah turned back to the house.

'Noah.'

Mr Noah looked round. The voice came again.

'Noah.'

'Is... is that you, God?'

'Yes.'

'It *was* all a dream, wasn't it?' Mr Noah asked anxiously. 'I mean about destroying the world and... and everything?'

'I'm afraid not.'

'Oh dear.'

'Now listen to me carefully, Noah. You're the only good man left in the world and I'm relying on you...'

And while Mr Noah stood in the middle of his farm in the middle of the night, God told him what he wanted him to do.

The following day, Mr Noah spoke to his family.

'Build an ark?' asked his eldest son, Shem.

'Yes,' said Mr Noah.

'Large enough for all of us, as well as two of every

animal, insect and bird?' asked his middle son, Ham.

'Yes.'

'You can't be serious, Dad,' said Japheth, his youngest son.

Mr Noah sighed.

'It was the onions he ate last night,' said Mrs Noah. 'And if it wasn't that, it was too much wine. I told him, but he wouldn't believe me. And if it wasn't the food or the drink, then it has to be too much sun.'

'We've never had such a good summer,' said Ham. 'It's been the driest for years. *Too* dry, if anything.'

'That's what makes all this talk of a flood such nonsense,' said Mrs Noah as she rose to clear the table.

'And if we don't get the harvest in soon, Father, the grapes will be over-ripe,' said Shem firmly.

It was true, and in the days that followed Mr Noah was too busy to worry about any flood. The sun beat down and the family turned nut-brown as they worked in the vineyard.

At odd times though, when he was busy picking grapes, or standing upright to ease his aching back, Mr Noah did think about what God had said, but he pushed such thoughts firmly to the back of his mind.

Late one evening, when Mr Noah was looking with satisfaction at the baskets filled to overflowing with grapes, and had just popped a particularly juicy, sun-ripened one into his mouth, God spoke to him again.

'Noah.'

Mr Noah almost choked.

'Noah, what have you done about building the ark?'

'Well, God,' Mr Noah began, 'I've been very busy, and I'm really very sorry but somehow it just slipped my mind...'

'The animals will be arriving soon, Noah.'

'Will they?' asked Mr Noah anxiously, and looked around, half expecting to see them marching up the track to his front door.

'Noah, I chose you out of all the people in the world. Don't let me down.'

That made Mr Noah feel perfectly dreadful. That evening after supper he spoke to his family.

'It wasn't the onions or the wine or the sun giving me bad dreams. It was God. We must start building a big boat, so that we'll be ready to leave when the flood comes.'

For a moment there was silence. Then Mrs Noah gave a shriek.

'Leave? Leave the farm?' She threw her apron over her head, sat down in a corner and burst into tears.

'Now look what you've done, Father,' said Ham, and Mr Noah sighed.

In the days that followed, the harvest was neglected as Mr Noah and his sons began building the ark according to the plans laid down by God. Mrs Noah and his son's wives began to pack.

No one believed Mr Noah's tale.

'I mean, why should God choose to speak to Mr Noah about important matters like building an ark and saving the animals?' said Mrs Noah as she bundled up their clothes. 'He's a good man, but he's not all that special. His carpentry's a nightmare and as for animals…! He runs a mile at the sight of a spider!'

'He's either made it up, got it wrong or is as mad as a hatter,' said Ham as he knocked nails into the wooden structure of the ark. 'And I think he's got it wrong. Stands to reason. He's six hundred years old. When you get to his age you're bound to muddle things up.'

As time went on Mr Noah also began to have doubts. Perhaps everyone else was right. Perhaps he was suffering from strain and overwork. Perhaps he had only imagined that God had spoken to him. After all, why should God speak to him? The work on the ark slowed down and then stopped as the family returned to their neglected vineyard.

It was the very last day of the harvest and the family were in the kitchen eating their midday meal. Mr Noah was just congratulating himself on a good crop, Shem was saying how lucky they'd been with the weather, and Mrs Noah was planning the big feast they would have that evening, when Japheth, white-faced and shaking, ran in. Pointing a trembling finger through the open door, he managed to whisper, 'F-father… look…!'

Mr Noah turned.

The track outside the house was full of animals. There were large animals and small ones, hairy and smooth. There were animals with tails and ones without. There were wild animals and tame ones,

good-looking and ugly. And not only animals. There
were reptiles and insects, beasts and birds. And not just
one of each. There were two of every kind, all forming
a long, long line down to the farmhouse.

A tap at the window was soon followed by a piercing

scream from Mrs Noah. Mr Noah turned. A large polar bear was looking in at them. Suddenly there was a great crash and the polar bear disappeared from view. Mr Noah picked up a stout stick, took a deep breath and went outside.

The polar bear lay stretched on the ground, while a second bear was busily fanning her with part of a broken chair.

'She can't take the heat, poor thing,' the second polar bear explained.

'That was my favourite chair!' Mr Noah groaned.

An important-looking lion with a fine golden mane strolled over. 'We've been informed by God that there's some kind of boat or ship around here. Is this the right place?'

'Yes. This is the right place. It's just that we're not quite ready…'

An emu stuck its head out from behind a tree. 'Is this the ark?' she asked in a sharp voice, peering at the farmhouse.

'No. It's just…'

'Doesn't look very watertight to me if it is.' The emu sniffed disapprovingly.

'The ark's not quite finished yet, but…'

'Well I hope the accommodation will be satisfactory. My husband and I are very fussy about where we stay.'

'It will be satisfactory,' said Mr Noah desperately. 'I assure you. Very satisfactory indeed…'

A large, hairy ape came round the corner of the

porch. 'I hope you're right,' he said in a menacing voice.

Mr Noah took a step backwards and fell into the remains of the chair, which promptly collapsed under him.

'Are you in charge here?' asked the lion in a disbelieving voice.

'Yes,' said Mr Noah, scrambling to his feet. 'That is… God's in charge really but I'm his deputy.'

'Well then, "deputy", how about some food, eh?' asked a jackal. 'We've all travelled a long way, and if we don't get something to eat, we might be tempted to eat you.' He snarled, showing a set of razor-sharp teeth, and the other animals laughed.

Mr Noah fled inside his house and shut the door. He turned to face his family, but they had run away to their rooms and locked themselves in.

'God?'

'Yes, Noah.'

'God, what shall I do?'

'You had better finish the ark.'

'Do I have to?' Mr Noah asked, watching in horror as two very black and very hairy spiders crept under the door.

'No. You don't have to.'

'Will you send the animals away then?'

God was silent for a moment.

'When I made you, Noah,' God said at last, 'I gave you freedom. The freedom to choose. You can do what I ask, or not. It is as *you* wish. I decided to save you and your family from the flood because you are a good man, the only good man in the world, but it's up to you. It's your choice. I'm offering you life, Noah, but you are free to refuse if you want.'

Mr Noah, keeping one eye firmly on the spiders, thought about what God had said. Then he went to his room, washed his face, combed his hair, put on a clean robe and called his family together.

'God and I have talked it over and I've decided to finish the ark.' He looked at his silent family. 'Now I'm just a foolish old man who isn't much good at anything, but for some reason, God's chosen me. He even asked me, very nicely, if I would do the job, and I said yes.'

'But you don't like animals...' Ham began.

'I don't, and I'm very sure the animals won't like me, and how we're all going to get along together is beyond me. But I'm sure God has it all worked out. What we've got to do now is build the ark before it's too late.'

'You mean, g-go out th-there?' Japheth asked in a small, scared voice.

'Yes,' said Mr Noah, trying to sound calm.

He walked to the door and took a deep breath.

'Please help me, God. I'm so scared, I'm shaking in my shoes.'

'Of course. You'll always have my help.'

'Thank you,' Mr Noah said, and went out alone to face the animals.

2

THE DOG'S TALE

Although Mr Noah was very grateful to God for deciding to save him and his family from the flood that would destroy the world, he did have a few worries.

'I'm not good with animals, God. Some people have a way with them, and some don't. I don't. To be honest with you, they scare me. And those that don't scare me plain terrify me. That's why I decided to grow grapes, rather than keep farm animals. Wouldn't an animal farmer suit your purpose better? Or a zoo-keeper?'

But God had every confidence in Mr Noah.

If Mr Noah was grateful to God, his family were less so.

'I don't like boats,' said Japheth gloomily. 'I get seasick.'

'It's not right God making me take a trip like this at my time of life,' grumbled Mrs Noah. 'Just when the farm was doing so nicely.'

'It seems a bit unfair on Father, too,' Ham added, 'at his great age.'

None of the animals arriving on the ark seemed grateful either. As Mr Noah welcomed them on board, complaints came thick and fast.

'Is *that* meant to be our watering-hole?' asked the hippopotamus when he was shown the small pool Mr Noah had built. 'You can't seriously expect us to wallow in that!'

'And where's the mud?' asked his wife, flopping into the water with such a splash that Mr Noah was soaked. 'Everyone knows you can't have a good wallow without mud.'

'The mud hasn't arrived yet,' Mr Noah explained. 'But Shem and Ham are down by the river digging it out right now.'

'Hmm,' said the hippopotamus, flopping into the pool after his wife and soaking Mr Noah for a second time.

The rest of the animals were just as bad.

'Say, Mr Noah!' called the pig, as Mr Noah was hurrying to his cabin to put on a dry robe. 'Honey, my wife, isn't too happy with her sty.'

'What's the matter with it?'

'The straw's smelly and my Honey has a very sensitive nose. And we would have liked to be more in the middle of the ark. Less likely to be seasick we've been told. But that's okay, we can live with that. The real problem is our neighbours. Did you *have* to put those two mean-looking scorpions right next door? It's given Honey a real fright.'

The only one who seemed at all content was Mr Noah's dog. Day after day she stayed close beside him as he welcomed the animals, insects and birds onto the ark and dealt with their complaints.

'It is very difficult for them, having to leave their homes,' Mr Noah sighed as he was getting ready for bed. 'I can understand how they feel. It's difficult for all of us.'

'They ought to be grateful to you,' said his dog. 'After all, you're giving them the chance of being saved from the flood.'

'It's not me they ought to be grateful to. It's God. He decides who's going to be saved.'

As Mr Noah's dog curled up at the foot of his bed, she thought about what Mr Noah had said. So far no other dogs had arrived on the ark. Did that mean that

God had decided to save her?

'Unlikely,' she thought. 'God will want to save two good-looking dogs, not a shabby old mongrel like me.' She sighed. It would be hard to leave Mr Noah. He was a kind, good man and she loved him very much.

'But perhaps he won't mind too much,' she reflected. 'He's got so many other animals to look after. I don't suppose he's given me a thought.'

But she was wrong. Mr Noah had thought about her. He had even spoken about her to God.

'I don't know what dogs you're thinking of saving, God, but could I put in a word for mine? I've had her for years and she's been loyal and faithful. She's a good guard dog as well, not that we need a guard dog on the ark.'

God did not answer.

'I know she's only a mongrel, but I'm very attached to her.'

God still did not answer.

'I really wouldn't bother you with such a small thing when you've so much else to do, and of course I'll accept whatever you decide, because I know it'll be all for the best, but still…'

'I need to save *two* of every living creature, Noah,' God said gently. 'And your dog doesn't have a mate.'

'I'm sure I could find another dog…'

'There's very little time. Your job is to welcome the animals onto the ark. Leave the choosing to me.'

'Oh,' said Mr Noah. 'Yes. Of course.'

The following day was hot and still, the sky black and threatening. Mr Noah's dog stood beside him as a steady stream of animals reported to Mr Noah, were ticked off his long list, and climbed on board the ark.

Late that afternoon the first spots of rain began to fall.

'It's started to rain!' called the eagle, flying into the great hall from the trapdoor set high up in the roof.

The animals fell silent. Then the emu shrieked, 'We're all going to drown!'

The ostrich tried to bury her head in the wooden floor of the hall and the elephant fainted, causing the ark to wobble violently.

'It's started to rain,' said Rachel, Shem's wife, opening the door to Mrs Noah's cabin.

'Well that's a good thing,' said Mrs Noah comfortably. 'The sooner we're afloat, the sooner the journey will be over and we can all go home.'

Mr Noah looked up at the sky. It was raining harder now and the light was fading.

'The animals will be worried,' he muttered and hurried off to the great hall.

His dog turned to follow, then stopped. In the fading light she could see two animals approaching. They looked, she thought with a sinking heart, like two dogs. Without waiting for them to come any closer, she jumped down from the ark and ran off.

It was very quiet away from the ark. The only sound was the pitter-pattering of rain on the leaves. The air felt thick and stuffy as if the world was holding its breath. Mr Noah's dog ran on into the thickening gloom.

It was pitch black by the time Mr Noah had quietened the animals. He looked round for his dog but could not see her anywhere. He ran all over the ark calling her name, then searched the entire boat twice through. She was gone. Mr Noah sat in his cabin and put his head in his hands.

'Where is she, God? Where has she gone?'

'She's all right, Noah. I'll look after her.'

Mr Noah was silent for a moment. Then he jumped off his bed.

'She's my dog and I'm going after her,' he protested. 'I'm sorry, God, but I can't leave her behind. I don't like to disobey you, but I'm afraid you'll have to find someone else to look after the animals if I don't come back in time. Shem, my eldest, is a good lad.'

And without another word he ran out of his cabin.

Mr Noah had never known such darkness. The sky was covered by thick clouds and the rain was pouring down. Mr Noah was soon soaked to the skin. His abandoned farmhouse, when he reached it, was welcome shelter and he thought he would stay there until daylight made his search easier. He pushed open the door and stepped into the kitchen.

With a loud bark, his dog flew at Mr Noah and knocked him backwards.

'It's all right,' Mr Noah said, laughing and hugging her tightly. 'It's all right. Did you think I'd go without you?'

'I couldn't bear to say goodbye,' said his dog. 'I never thought you'd come to find me.'

'Come on now, let's get back to the ark.'

'But God doesn't want me. He wants two of every animal and there's only one of me.'

'There's only one of me too,' said a tired voice, 'so we'd better go together.'

Mr Noah and his dog turned. A tired and very wet dog stood on the threshold.

He limped into the room. 'I do hope I'm not too late but it's taken me a long time to get here. I ran into a snare and hurt my leg. I was just about ready to give up when I heard your voices.'

He stopped. 'I'm very hungry and very tired but very pleased to meet you. It's Mr Noah, isn't it?'

'Yes,' said Mr Noah, bending down to pat him.

'I don't understand,' Mr Noah's dog said, as they made their way back to the ark. 'You can't want us. You've already got two dogs on the ark. I saw them. That's why I ran away.'

Mr Noah laughed. 'You must have seen the two wolves. They came soon after the rain began. In the dim light you must have mistaken them.' He hugged both the dogs. 'You're the ones God has chosen and I'm delighted. I should never have doubted.'

And as he strode towards the welcoming lights of the ark, the two dogs ran happily at his heels.

3

THE TORTOISE'S TALE

For many days now the animals had been arriving at the ark which God had told Mr Noah to build. Large ones, small ones, smooth ones, hairy ones, animals, insects and birds, they arrived two by two in order to be saved from the flood. As they walked, ran, crawled and slithered up the gangplank, Mr Noah ticked them off his long list.

By the time the two cheetahs raced up the gangplank, Mr Noah's list was almost complete and the rain had begun to fall, thick round drops out of a heavily laden sky.

'We're not too late are we?' one of them panted.

'No,' said Mr Noah. 'I've been expecting you. You're very welcome.'

Inside the ark the latest arrivals stared in amazement at the number of animals, insects and birds thronging the great hall. The noise was tremendous.

'Hello,' said the donkey, 'forgive my ignorance, but

who are you? I don't think we've met.'

'We're cheetahs.'

'Oh really,' said the donkey politely. 'How interesting. I've met so many strange and wonderful animals on this ark. Cheetahs. That's a new one to me. What do you do, if you don't mind my asking?'

'What do you mean?'

'Well, so many of the animals here seem able to *do* things. It's quite amazing. Just look at the giraffe with his wonderful long neck. So useful to see things from high up. The herons can stand on one leg and the peacock has a most beautiful tail. Everyone seems to be clever at something except me. I'm very dull and boring.'

'We run,' said the cheetah. 'Like the wind.'

'In fact,' said his mate, 'without wishing to boast, we run faster than any animal in the world.'

'Really,' said the donkey, admiringly.

A crowd of animals had gathered.

'The fastest animals in the world?' snarled the leopard. 'Prove it.'

'I always thought *we* were the fastest animals in the world,' murmured one of the gazelles.

'So did I,' said the other gazelle. She eyed the cheetahs nervously. 'Especially when there's a cheetah behind us.'

The cheetahs smiled. 'This could be a most enjoyable trip,' said the first cheetah, licking his lips.

'There's to be NO eating of other animals while on

board,' said the lion in a loud voice.

'Who said?' demanded the cheetah.

'Mr Noah. I am his deputy.'

'And I'm his other deputy,' said the tiger.

'It's one of the rules,' explained the donkey.

'It's a good rule,' squawked the chicken.

'*That's* a matter of opinion,' said the fox.

One of the kangaroos bounded up. 'While we're on the subject of speed...'

'I thought we were on the subject of food,' said the fox.

'...we're reckoned pretty fast runners,' the kangaroo said brightly.

'Why don't we have a race?' the elephant suggested. 'To find out which of the animals *is* the fastest.'

'I'll be the judge,' said the lion grandly.

'Is there a rule about holding a race?' asked the donkey, but nobody took any notice, for the birds were busy flying up to the rafters and the animals pressing themselves to the sides of the great hall in order to clear a space.

A long way away from the ark, two tortoises were sheltering from the rain under a stone.

'Don't you think we ought to be getting on?' asked the first tortoise anxiously.

'There's no rush,' said the second tortoise. She peered out. 'It's very wet out there.'

'That's because it's raining.'

'I know that,' said the first tortoise. He closed his eyes.

'You can't go to sleep now!' said the second tortoise. 'At the rate we're going, the world will be flooded before we reach the ark!'

The second tortoise opened her eyes. 'More haste, less speed,' she said, then shut her eyes again.

Safe on the ark, Mr Noah had just discovered that the tortoises were missing.

'We must search the ark. They could have slipped past without my knowing.'

'We ought to close the doors, Father,' Shem objected. 'Otherwise the ark will be flooded.'

'This might just be a shower,' said Mr Noah hopefully. 'And we can't leave the tortoises behind.'

'If it's a choice between saving the tortoises and drowning, I know which I'd choose,' muttered Shem.

Inside the great hall, the animals who were entering the race were lining up.

'Three times round, and no pushing, biting or scratching,' said the lion.

'Are those more rules?' asked the donkey.

'On your marks... get set... go!'

Everyone cheered and the race was on.

'Stop!' shouted the lion. 'Stop!' He walked up to the ostrich.

'You are not an animal, you are a bird. Therefore you are disqualified from this race.'

The ostrich's eyes filled with tears. 'Oh please let me join in!' she begged.

The lion shook his great head and the ostrich slunk away, sniffing.

'Mean, I call it,' squawked the parrot. 'What harm would there have been in letting the ostrich race?'

'My dear parrot,' said the lion in his grandest manner. 'This race is to find the fastest land animal. Therefore only animals can take part. Rules are rules.'

'I thought there would be a rule somewhere,' said the donkey, satisfied, and the race began again.

Inside his cabin, Mr Noah was talking to God.

'It would be terrible if tortoises were to die out because they didn't arrive in time to travel on the ark. But what can I do? They could be anywhere.'

'Trust me,' said God. 'I haven't forgotten the tortoises. But they may need some help.'

'From me?'

'From you and the animals.'

Just then, Mr Noah's three sons burst into his cabin.

'The tortoises aren't anywhere on the ark,' said Shem.

'The water's coming right up the gangplank!' Ham exclaimed.

'You'll never believe what the animals are doing!' Japheth shouted. 'They're having a race!'

Mr Noah looked up. 'A race...?' he said. 'Now I wonder...'

In the hall the race had just ended.

'You cheated!' said the kangaroo crossly.

'Are you calling me a cheat?' asked the cheetah.

'Cheat by name and cheat by nature.'

The cheetah circled the kangaroo, snarling.

'Now, now,' said the elephant. 'No fighting on the ark.'

'Another of Mr Noah's rules,' explained the donkey to anyone who was listening.

'We'll have one deciding round between the cheetah and the kangaroo,' said the lion.

Mr Noah entered the hall. 'Animals!'

'On your marks... get set...'

'I need your help!'

'What do you want our help for?' asked the panther bluntly. 'I thought you and God had it all sewn up between you.'

'The tortoises are missing.'

'That's their problem,' said the panther. 'They shouldn't be so slow.'

'*We* got here on time,' said one of the snails. 'And no

one could call us fast animals.'

'You're not animals at all,' said the fox. 'You're… you're…'

'Food,' said the eagle.

The snails went into their shells.

'On your marks… get set…' said the lion once more.

'Wait!' said Mr Noah. 'I have an idea.'

Far away from the ark, the two tortoises plodded on. They were wet, cold and miserable.

'Why don't we hibernate?' asked the second tortoise. 'Find some nice dry shelter somewhere and go to sleep until it's all over.'

'There aren't any nice dry shelters,' said the first tortoise. 'Or there won't be, soon. Come on slowcoach.'

The second tortoise sighed. 'You know, you're the nearest thing to a speedy tortoise I've ever met.'

Heads down, feet slipping and sliding, the tortoises slowly struggled on and did not notice the eagle, flying high above them. The eagle paused in mid-flight, circled once, twice, then turned on his wing and flew away.

'I've found them, Mr Noah,' he called, flying in through the trapdoor high up in the roof of the ark.

Mr Noah and the animals left the great hall and crowded round the entrance.

'Are you ready?' asked Mr Noah.

The cheetah and the kangaroo nodded their heads.

'Then…' said Mr Noah, 'on your marks… get set… go!'

To cheers from the animals, the eagle flew off,

showing the way to the cheetah and the kangaroo.

The cheetah reached the tortoises first.

'Hello,' said the first tortoise. 'If you're looking for the ark, you're going in the wrong direction.'

'I'm looking for you,' said the cheetah. 'You'll have to hurry or you'll be too late. The water is rising.'

'We're coming as fast as we can.'

'Could you climb on my back?' asked the cheetah. 'I run like the wind.'

The tortoises looked up at the cheetah, considered for a moment, then shook their heads. And they were still all standing there when the kangaroo arrived.

'All right,' said the kangaroo. 'You win. You *are* the fastest animal.'

'I might be able to run fast,' said the cheetah. 'But how do I get the tortoises safely to the ark? They can't climb on my back.'

The kangaroo looked at the tortoises and smiled. 'Leave it to me,' she said.

Back on the ark, Mr Noah was staring at the rising level of the water.

'You'll have to close the doors, Father!' said Shem urgently.

'Not until the tortoises arrive,' Mr Noah said stubbornly.

There was a stirring in the air. The eagle flew down and landed at Mr Noah's feet.

'Phew, it's wet out there,' he said, shaking his dripping feathers.

'Are they coming?' Mr Noah asked anxiously.

'Oh yes,' said the eagle. 'They're coming all right, although why God made wingless animals in the first place, I'll never know. Now if the tortoises each had a decent pair of wings, there wouldn't have been all this fuss in the first place.'

The cheetah came first, walking slowly and wearily. As he entered the ark, the animals cheered.

'I award you, cheetah, land speed record,' said the lion.

'I might be the fastest,' said the cheetah, 'but we all have our uses.'

'Where are the tortoises?' Mr Noah asked as the kangaroo bounded onto the ark.

A head popped out of the kangaroo's pouch.

'Here,' said the first tortoise.

'Here,' said the second tortoise. She turned to the kangaroo. 'Thank you for a very comfortable journey.'

God himself closed the great doors of the ark just as the water began to lap at the entrance. The ark rocked and the wooden frame creaked. Animals, insects, humans and birds fell silent. Then the eagle flew into the great hall.

'The ark,' he called in a loud voice, 'is afloat.'

4

THE GORILLA'S TALE

Once the ark was afloat, everyone began to settle down for the voyage.

'After all,' said the cow placidly, 'we're all in the same boat, so we'd better learn how to muck in together.'

'I've no wish to "muck in" with anyone,' said the goose, holding up her nose. 'In my opinion this entire venture has been badly managed from the start.'

'I couldn't agree more,' said the peacock. 'I asked for first-class accommodation but apparently there isn't any. Mr Noah said that God hadn't told him to provide it. Quite shocking!'

'In my opinion, Mr Noah is a bit too fond of blaming God,' said the goose.

'No one asked for your opinion,' muttered the cockroach.

The goose ignored this. 'Didn't Mr Noah have *any* say in building the ark? Let's face it, God can't have much experience in boat-building.'

'Neither has Mr Noah,' said the peacock. 'When I arrived he was putting the door in upside down.'

The goose sniggered. 'Well in *my* opinion...' she began, but at that moment the goat ran bleating into the hall.

'Save me! Oh save me! It's after me!'

'Who's after you?' asked the cow.

'The... the... monster!'

'I didn't know there were any monsters on board,' said the donkey in an interested voice.

The goat was trembling violently and uttering little bleating cries.

'Now just calm down, dear, and tell us all about it,' said the cow.

'It... it was black... and... and hairy,' the goat began.

'Are you referring to me?' asked the spider spinning down on a fine thread from the rafters.

'Of course not,' bleated the goat. 'This was enormous... and it walked on two great legs and had two long arms and a horrible face.'

The fox grinned. 'Are you sure you're not referring to our host, Mr Noah?' he asked. 'He walks on two legs and has two arms.' He thought for a moment. 'I wouldn't consider his face *horrible* exactly, not as human faces go, but there's no accounting for tastes.'

'No it wasn't Mr Noah!' said the goat. 'It was a monster!'

'I'd like to see a monster,' said the donkey.

Just then there was a footfall behind him and he

turned round. The goat bleated loudly, the emu had hysterics, the ostrich fainted, the goose flew up and down in a panic, while the cause of all the fuss stared at the animals with black, unblinking eyes, then shambled off.

'Wh-what was it?' asked the goose breathlessly.

'Enough to give one nightmares,' said the peacock, fanning himself vigorously with his tail.

'Was that the monster?' asked the donkey.

'No,' said the chimpanzee, swinging down from a beam. 'That's the gorilla.'

'Oh. One of *your* relations is it?' snapped the emu.

'Only distantly,' said the chimpanzee.

'I don't care what his name is,' said the goat. 'If I'd known creatures like that were going to be on this trip, I wouldn't have come.'

'You'd rather have drowned, I suppose,' the fox murmured drily.

'Well I think it's quite horrible and should never have been allowed on the ark,' said the peacock firmly.

And that was the opinion of most of the animals, insects and birds.

It was not that the two gorillas did anything to upset the animals, it was just that they were always there: dark menacing shapes disappearing round corners, large flat faces staring from the back of the great hall, hairy black bodies turning up in unexpected places before shambling slowly away.

'It makes life very uncomfortable,' said the emu. 'I really think someone should complain to Mr Noah.'

'I agree,' said the goose.

'Me too,' quacked the duck, who did not really know what was being discussed but liked to agree with the goose as it made him feel important.

But when Mr Noah heard the animals' complaints, he shook his head.

'I'm sorry, but God told me to take two of every living creature—other than fish—onto the ark and we must all learn to get along with one another.'

'*They* should learn to get along with *us*,' said the goat firmly.

'Have you tried talking to the gorillas?' Mr Noah asked mildly.

'Talking to them?' said the peacock. 'Me? You must be joking!'

'May I suggest that if there's any talking to be done, then you should do it, Mr Noah,' said the lion. 'God saw fit to make you our captain, our fearless leader, and it's your duty to protect us weak animals from danger.' He smiled as he said this, showing a mouth full of strong, well-sharpened teeth.

'I thought you'd say that,' muttered Mr Noah and retreated to the safety of his cabin.

'You see, God,' Mr Noah said, 'I'm scared of the gorillas too, as I expect you know. They are so very big and so very strong and so very hairy.' He shuddered. 'They might be angry if I speak to them, and an angry gorilla doesn't bear thinking about.' He closed his eyes. '*Two* angry gorillas would be even worse.'

With that he climbed into bed, but it was a long time before he went to sleep. He was woken by a loud noise. The ark shuddered violently and Mr Noah found himself thrown out of bed and across the room.

The noise had woken most of the animals in the great hall. As Mr Noah entered, the ark shuddered again, then started to tilt. Animals began sliding to the far end and the birds rose from their perches and flew up to the rafters.

'Hey… whoa…!' called the horse, sliding past the giraffe.

'Have we reached land?' squealed the rat, its claws skittering on the floor.

'As your deputy, Mr Noah,' said the lion, clinging tightly to a wooden beam, 'I think I ought to be informed when the boat behaves in this irregular manner. It's very... very... undignified...'

The ark shuddered once more, the lion lost his grip and crashed into the tiger.

'I don't know what's going on,' said Mr Noah, 'but I'll try and find out.'

'Well I blame it on those gorillas,' said the goat. 'They're probably jumping up and down at the other end of the ark to make it tip up.'

Mr Noah climbed the steps that led to the trapdoor in the roof and peered out. What he saw made him turn pale and he climbed back inside.

'The ark,' he said, 'seems to have run aground.'

'Does that mean that it's all over?' asked the pig, hopefully. 'Say, Mr Noah, have we reached land?'

'No,' said Mr Noah. 'I'm afraid we've hit something.'

'I knew it!' shrieked the emu. 'We've hit an iceberg! We're all going to drown!'

'Nonsense,' said the polar bear. 'There's no ice around here. It's far too warm.' And he fanned himself with his great paw.

'I think the ark has become trapped between the peaks of two mountains,' said Mr Noah.

'How long before it's smashed to pieces?' the monkey asked gloomily.

'We *are* going to drown!' cried the emu. 'We're trapped and we're all going to drown!'

The ostrich gave a great sob and tried to bury his head in the wooden floor.

'Nonsense,' said Mr Noah, with a certainty he was far from feeling. 'God won't let us drown.'

'Then why did he let us get stuck on these rocks?' asked the jackal in a smooth voice.

The ark shuddered once more.

'I'm going to try and push us off,' said Mr Noah.

'Have you any oars?' asked the beaver.

'Well, no,' said Mr Noah. 'God never said anything about oars.'

'You see?' said the goose to whoever was listening. 'Blaming God *all* the time.'

Mr Noah again climbed out onto the roof of the ark. The wind was blowing furiously, the rain lashing down. The roof was very slippery. Mr Noah made his way to the end that was wedged and pushed against the rock. Nothing happened. He pushed harder. Then he called his three sons and their wives and they all pushed but it was no use. The ark was stuck fast.

Inside the hall several of the animals were beginning to feel seasick.

'This is a terrible way to travel,' said the camel. 'Give me the desert any time.'

'I always said it would end in tears,' said the monkey in an I-told-you-so voice.

Up on the roof, an exhausted Mr Noah was talking

to God. 'You can't mean it to end like this, God,' he said. 'Not after all the trouble you've taken to save us. Please tell me what to do.'

The trapdoor opened.

'Uh, sorry to bother you, Mr Noah,' said a hesitant voice, 'but perhaps we could help?'

Mr Noah turned and almost fell off the roof, for right behind him stood two very large, very black and very hairy gorillas.

'We don't like to interfere,' said the gorilla's wife in a quiet, earnest voice, 'we're not animals who put ourselves forward you know. Do feel free to tell us to go away.'

'No,' said Mr Noah, 'no, please don't go. I think you could be the answer to a prayer. Could you... would you... push us off the rocks?'

'We can try,' said the gorilla. 'What do you think, petal?'

His wife nodded her head vigorously. 'Yes indeed. We can certainly try.'

So taking a firm grip of the floor with their massive feet, the two gorillas pressed their great arms against the rocks and grunted.

The ark creaked and groaned. Then, with a loud sucking sound, it floated free. The movement was so sudden that the gorillas almost overbalanced.

They came down from the roof to loud applause.

'Three cheers for the gorillas!' the elephant trumpeted.

'No… no… it was nothing,' said the gorilla, trying to hide behind Mr Noah.

'Hip, hip…!'

'Please don't… it's all very embarrassing,' said the gorilla's wife.

'We are… hmm… very sorry if we've given you any cause to think we didn't… um…' the lion began.

'No, not at all,' the gorilla assured him.

'You see, it's just because you look like monsters,' said the donkey. 'At least, that's what the goat said, but as I've never seen a monster, I can't tell if she's right.'

'We knew how you felt,' said the gorilla's wife. 'That's why we tried not to bother you. We're really very peace-loving animals you know. We wouldn't hurt a fly.'

'Thanks,' said the fly.

'Thank you,' said Mr Noah. 'You saved the ark from sinking.'

'Nonsense,' said the eagle, from his perch high up in the roof.

'What do you mean?'

'If you had only waited until the water had risen some more, the ark would have floated off the rocks without any other help at all.'

'Why didn't you say so?' demanded Mr Noah.

'You didn't ask,' said the eagle, and closed his eyes.

'But if the gorillas hadn't come to the rescue, we'd all still have been scared of them,' said the donkey.

'That's very true,' said Mr Noah. 'Perhaps it's taught us all a lesson.' He went over to the gorilla and took his hand. 'Not to judge by appearances.'

Later that night, as Mr Noah was about to go to sleep, he suddenly had a thought.

'You knew that the ark would float off the rocks if we did nothing about it, didn't you God?' he demanded.

'I don't tell you everything, Noah,' said God.

5

THE FOX'S TALE

The first faint streaks of daylight showed a grey, wet world as the rain, which God had sent, poured down from overcast skies. Floating in the sea of rainwater was the ark, bobbing up and down at the mercy of the wind and waves.

Inside the ark most of the animals were still fast asleep. But as dawn broke, the cock got to his feet, filled his lungs with air, and crowed.

'Cock-a-doodle-doo! Wakey-wakey!'

He turned to his wife.

'Don't you think my voice sounds rather fine this morning?'

His wife, the hen, nodded.

The cock puffed out his chest. 'Cock-a-doodle-doo! Time to get up you sleepy heads!'

There was a stirring among the animals in the great hall.

'Can't you pipe down?' muttered the tiger.

'Cock-a-doodle-doo!'

'Cock-a-doodle-doo yourself,' snapped the fox. 'Stop that noise or I'll stop it for you!'

He bared his teeth and jumped at the cock, who gave a loud squawk and leaped out of the way. The fox laughed.

'Did you see that?' said the cock. 'Violence! I've been threatened with violence.'

'It's your fault for crowing,' said the tiger unsympathetically. 'It's all very well on a farm, but this is the ark and I don't see any need to get up early.'

'Neither do I,' said the crocodile. 'Sleeping helps pass the time.'

'It's not even day yet,' grumbled the goat.

'Yes it is,' said the cock. 'It's a fine day.'

'It's not a fine day,' said the skylark from high up in the roof. 'It's another wet one.'

'Cock-a-doodle-doo!' crowed the cock.

'Well I'm going back to sleep,' said the goat,

'and if you start crowing again, I'll, I'll...'

'Eat you?' suggested the fox.

'I don't eat animals. I only eat grass and leaves.'

'But I don't,' said the fox, licking his lips. 'I'd be happy to take care of the cock for you. Very happy indeed. And the hen. Especially the hen, who's a nice, plump little bird. Just as I like them.'

He pounced at the hen who squawked loudly.

'Here, you leave my wife alone!' shouted the cock. 'Bully!'

'If you're calling names,' said the fox, 'then your crowing makes you sound like a... like a strangulated duck!'

'Quack,' said the duck. 'Did someone mention my name?'

The cock bristled. 'I've never been so insulted in my life!'

He puffed up his chest and crowed as loudly as he could. 'Cock-a-doodle-doo! Cock-a-doodle-doo!'

His crowing brought Mr Noah, half-dressed and only half-awake, into the hall.

'Is anything the matter?' he asked.

'Yes there is,' said the cock. 'That fox attacked me and my wife.'

'It was only a joke,' said the fox.

'Funny sort of joke. He said he would eat us.'

The tiger opened one eye. 'It was only because the cock *would* insist on crowing in the middle of the night.'

'It's not the middle of the night,' snapped the cock.

'It's early morning. Cocks always welcome the dawn by crowing.'

'If I was the dawn,' said the fox, 'I'd do without your welcome.'

'Now fox,' said Mr Noah, 'You know the rules of the ark. No eating one another on the voyage.'

'Rules are made to be broken,' murmured the fox.

Mr Noah eyed him sternly. 'These rules are for the good of everyone on board.'

'But it's *such* a temptation, Mr Noah,' the fox said, casting longing looks at the cock and the hen. 'Just imagine having your favourite food walking in front of you when you're starving.'

'But you're not starving,' said Mr Noah.

'No, but it's not the same eating the food you give us,' said the fox. He grinned. 'I like my food live. Gets my taste buds working and the hunt adds to the pleasure of eating.' He licked his lips. 'It's really very difficult seeing two such delicious morsels of food strutting around. And it's very dangerous,' he added, 'the cock waking me up by crowing. I mean, I might eat him without realizing it, while I'm still half-asleep.'

'Then you'd best go and sleep on the other side of the hall, far away from temptation,' said Mr Noah.

The fox sighed and slunk away.

But the following morning he was up well before the cock. He crept round the edge of the hall until he was right outside the hen-coop.

The cock woke up, looked at the thin shaft of

daylight filtering in through the trapdoor high up in the roof, got to his feet and filled his lungs.

The fox leaped forwards, snapping his teeth. The cock jumped high in the air and gave a loud shriek.

'Just like a strangulated duck,' said the fox laughing, and slunk back to his lair on the far side of the hall.

The cock was furious. 'Something ought to be done!' he shouted.

His shouting woke the tiger, who roared, 'Can't you let a poor old animal sleep in peace?'

'You're one of Mr Noah's deputies,' said the cock, 'so get off your lazy backside and do something!'

'All right.' The tiger got to his feet. 'Anything for a quiet life.'

The fox protested, 'But I only meant it as a joke!'

'I know that. In fact between you and me, I wouldn't be too sorry if something did happen to that cock.'

'Well then.'

'But the thing is that it's just not on. It's letting Mr Noah down.'

The fox shrugged. 'What's Mr Noah got to do with it?'

'He saved us from being drowned in the flood.'

'He didn't do that. God did.'

'All right,' said the tiger patiently. 'It's letting God down.'

The following day, when Mr Noah was cleaning the lower deck of the ark, he found a single white feather lying on the ground. A little way on he found another feather. A trail of feathers led right round the ark.

He went to the great hall.

'What does all this mean?' he asked sternly.

'Oh Mr Noah,' squawked the hen. 'Mr Noah, it was the fox!'

The fox blinked. 'Me?'

'He chased me right round the ark and tore out those feathers. I nearly had heart failure I was so scared!'

'But I didn't,' the fox protested. 'I didn't do anything.'

'He said he'd eat me next time he caught me.'

Mr Noah turned to the fox. 'Well?'

'She's lying,' said the fox.

'Why should she lie? Someone's torn out her feathers and she's obviously upset. I'm going to move the cock and the hen to a different part of the ark so they'll be well out of harm's way.'

For a few days there was peace. The cock and the hen were in such a remote part of the ark that the cock's crowing did not wake the animals, and no further complaints were made about the fox.

Then one evening, both the cock and the hen went to find Mr Noah.

'He's at it again,' said the cock.

'Why, what's happened?'

'Go on,' said the cock. 'Tell him.'

'I was just having a scratch around for some seed when that fox popped his head over the edge of my coop and leered. "That's it," he said, "fatten yourself up. All the tastier for me." ' The hen sniffed. 'I'm so upset, it's stopped me from laying.'

'You should lock him up,' said the cock. 'He's a public menace.'

'All right,' said Mr Noah. 'Leave it with me.'

But the cock and the hen had plenty more to say before they could be persuaded to go back to their coop, leaving Mr Noah free to speak to God.

'What shall I do, God?' he asked. 'For if the fox does eat the hen, then all the other animals will start eating each other. By the time the floods go down and the ark finds land there'll be no animals left to repopulate the world. I don't like the idea of locking up the fox, but what else can I do?'

God was silent for a moment.

'It's not as simple as it appears,' he said at last.

'Isn't it?'

'Do nothing for the moment, Noah. Just keep your eyes and your ears open and then you will find out the truth.'

'Yes, God. And I'll watch that fox and make sure he doesn't get near the chickens.'

'Watch the chickens, too.'

'Yes, of course I will. To make sure they're safe.'

It was while Mr Noah was on his way to pay a visit to the cock and the hen that he heard them talking.

'So the next time I say that the fox grabbed hold of my wing, is that it?' asked the hen.

'Yes, but say that he let it go when I rushed up,' said the cock.

'He let it go when you rushed up,' repeated the hen.

'That'll fix him!' said the cock and crowed loudly.

Mr Noah stepped forwards. 'I heard what you both said. You've been lying, haven't you?'

The cock and the hen hung their heads. 'Well, yes,' they admitted.

'Why?'

'It was too much of a temptation,' the hen explained. 'It gave us a chance to get our own back. After all, he *would* eat us if he could.'

'A lot of animals on the ark would eat each other. But as I've explained, you've all been specially chosen by God and you've agreed not to eat each other while you remain here.'

The cock and the hen looked at one another.

'That wasn't the only reason, was it?'

'Well, no,' said the cock. 'That fox was very rude about my crowing. He said… he said that I sounded like a strangulated duck.'

'It was a very rude and unkind thing to say,' said the hen.

'So you thought you would teach the fox a lesson, is that it?'

'Yes.'

'Come along,' said Mr Noah. 'I think you owe the fox an apology, don't you? And—if I might make a suggestion—why don't you stop crowing first thing in the morning?'

'I can't do that,' said the cock. 'I must crow. It's in my nature.'

'It's in the fox's nature to hunt for food,' said Mr Noah gently. 'And he's agreed not to on this voyage.'

The cock said nothing.

'How would you feel about crowing at some time other than first thing in the morning? Perhaps when it's time for food? I can't see that the animals would mind that.'

'All right,' said the cock.

The animals agreed and, for the rest of the voyage, the cock only crowed at mealtimes and everyone was happy.

6
THE CAMEL'S TALE

When Mr Noah was building the ark, God told him to pay special attention to the living quarters of the animals, insects and birds.

'I want the creatures I save from the flood to be as comfortable as possible during the voyage,' said God.

Mr Noah had given the matter a lot of thought and was rather pleased with the plans he had worked out, especially as he had no idea what most of the animals looked like.

So when one of the two camels arrived on board the ark, Mr Noah welcomed him and showed him to his quarters.

'I think you will like it,' he said as he led the way to the lower deck. 'It is a bit cramped I'm afraid—not like your home in the desert—but you should both be fairly comfortable.'

'Both?' queried the camel. 'What do you mean, both?'

'Well, your wife, the other camel,' Mr Noah said, surprised. 'I assume she'll be here very soon.'

'I don't know what you are talking about,' said the camel haughtily.

'But God has arranged for there to be two of every animal on the ark.'

'No one said anything to me about it, and I'm not at all sure I like the idea.'

A short while later, Mr Noah was welcoming a second camel onto the ark.

'Your husband is already here. I've shown him to his quarters.'

'Husband? I didn't know I had one.'

'Well,' Mr Noah began rather uncomfortably, 'most of the animals arrived here in twos. In fact I was a bit surprised when your husband arrived by himself because God insists that there are two of every animal, insect and bird on board the ark.'

'Hmm,' said the second camel, drily.

'I'm also a bit surprised because… Well, you'll see for yourself.'

He led the way to the first camel's sleeping quarters.

'There you are.'

The two camels stared at one another.

'Who,' asked the first camel, 'is this?'

'It's the second camel,' said Mr Noah.

'That creature is not a camel.'

'I could say the same about you,' said the second camel.

'How dare you say I'm not a camel! I am, as it happens, a dromedary, which is a highly superior camel, I'll have you know.'

'Well, if it comes to that, I'm also a superior camel. I am a Bactrian.'

'Never heard of them!'

Mr Noah looked nervously from one camel to the other. 'But you are both camels. I mean, you've both got humps.'

'That,' said the dromedary, 'is a matter of opinion.'

'Indeed,' said the Bactrian. 'If it comes to humps, I think you'll agree that I have the advantage. I, after all, have *two* humps. You only have the *one*.'

'Better to have one perfect hump than two inferior ones.'

The two camels glared at one another.

'Well,' said Mr Noah nervously, 'I'll just leave you two to… er… make friends with one another.' With that, he fled.

'Has there been some mistake, God?' he asked.

'No,' said God. 'There's been no mistake.'

'But I don't think they like each other very much.'

'They will, in time.'

But as time went on, the two camels appeared to dislike each other more and more.

'It's very common to have two humps,' said the dromedary. 'One is far more elegant.'

The Bactrian looked at him pityingly. 'I really don't know how you manage with only one hump. I wouldn't feel complete without my two.'

Both went, separately, to Mr Noah and demanded that they be given quarters at opposite ends of the ark.

'I'm sorry but there's just no room,' said Mr Noah. 'Do please try to get on together.'

'Get on? With that… that misshapen beast?' asked the dromedary.

'You must be joking!' said the Bactrian.

The two camels only spoke to each other when they thought of fresh insults, and at night-time they bit and kicked each other in their sleeping quarters. It was a nightmare for the animals who slept near them and they soon complained.

'It's bad enough having to sleep near animals who grunt, snort, squeak and snore, let alone those who fight all night,' the lion grumbled. 'There's a lot of unrest, Mr Noah, and I suggest you do something about it pretty quickly.'

'Oh dear. I did think that the camels might have learned to get on with each other by now.'

Mr Noah spoke to the camels, but it wasn't much use.

'Well, I'm sorry,' said the Bactrian, 'but I didn't start it. It's that one-humped monstrosity you should be talking to, not me.'

'No one mentioned sharing my quarters with a shaggy-haired, two-humped freak!' retorted the dromedary.

'When God created camels, he must have experimented with you and discovered that two humps were best!' the Bactrian shouted.

'*You* were the experiment. *I* was the finished product!'

Mr Noah hurried away.

'I shall have to separate them, shan't I, God?'

'You must do what you think best, Noah.'

'They do seem to hate each other so.'

'Hate? Do you think it's hate?'

'Well it's certainly not love,' Mr Noah retorted, and went to find some other living quarters for the Bactrian.

Although separating the two camels meant that everyone slept more peacefully at night, it did nothing to improve the atmosphere on the ark during the day, for both camels carried on their war. The animals, insects and birds on the ark grew sick of their constant fighting.

'You're both camels, aren't you?' asked the fox. 'So why can't you get on? I could understand the hyena and myself not getting on well, but surely you two have a lot more in common than the hyena and I.'

'But I do get on with you, fox,' said the hyena. 'I find you a very witty and amusing animal.'

'Do you really? Thank you very much. I find you quite pleasant too.'

The dromedary glared at the fox. 'First, I am not a hyena and have no wish to be. Second, I am not a fox and have even less wish in that direction, for I find you a very frivolous sort of animal. Third…' he broke off. 'I've forgotten what the third is.'

The Bactrian laughed nastily. 'Going soft in the head. It's the one hump you know.'

'I know that both you camels give me the hump,' said the monkey sourly.

'A hump is a very odd thing to have,' the jackdaw said thoughtfully. 'What do you keep in it?'

'I have a hump,' said the snail. 'But it's my shell. It's very useful because I can squeeze myself under it if it rains.'

'Then why aren't you squeezed under it now?' asked the jackdaw. 'It's raining, isn't it?'

'Not in here it's not.'

The jackdaw turned to the camels. 'Do you squeeze yourselves into your humps when it rains?'

'Of course not,' said the dromedary. 'I store food in my hump.'

The Bactrian smiled sweetly. 'I can store twice as much food as him, for I've two humps for storage.'

The dromedary kicked the Bactrian, who turned and bit the dromedary. Order was only restored when Mr Noah sent both animals to their sleeping quarters.

'What am I going to do with them, God?'

'Stop worrying, Noah.'

'That's all very well, but they're upsetting the other animals.'

For a few days neither camel was heard or seen in the great hall of the ark, much to everyone's relief.

'Perhaps Mr Noah's locked them up,' said the fox hopefully.

'Perhaps they're plotting how to kill each other,' said the yak.

'Perhaps they've already done it, which is why they're so quiet,' said the rat.

Just then the dromedary entered the hall and the animals gasped. For his hump, which had always been quite large, was now enormous, and the dromedary had to walk quite slowly and carefully in order not to overbalance.

The rat sniggered, the yak snorted, the fox guffawed, then all the animals, insects and birds inside the great hall burst out laughing. The dromedary took

one disdainful look at them, turned around—with great difficulty—and walked off.

'What on earth does he think he's doing?' asked the jackdaw.

'Whatever it is, he looks quite ridiculous,' said the fox.

Some days later, Ham, who was giving the larger animals their food, came running.

'Father, Father, you must come at once!'

Mr Noah hurried after Ham to the Bactrian's sleeping quarters. He looked down at the camel, lying on her bed of straw and was shocked. Her two humps had shrunk away and the flesh hung loosely on her back. Beside her was her untouched food.

'Are you ill?' Mr Noah asked.

The Bactrian looked at him weakly. 'No, not ill,' she said, and burst into tears.

Mr Noah had a long talk with God, then went in search of the dromedary.

'The Bactrian is dying. She won't eat.'

'More fool her. What do you expect me to do about it?'

'I don't know that I want you to *do* anything. I just thought you ought to know.'

'Oh,' said the dromedary.

Late that afternoon one end of the ark began to shake violently. Mr Noah went to investigate, but found his way barred. The dromedary's hump was firmly wedged in the doorway which led to the Bactrian's sleeping quarters.

'I'm stuck! Help me! Please help!'

In the end it took the combined efforts of Mr Noah, Ham, Shem, Japheth, both rhinoceros and one hippopotamus to push the dromedary through the door into the Bactrian's sleeping quarters.

The Bactrian tried to get to her feet but could only look up as the dromedary towered over her, his ungainly hump bruised and sore.

'I'm sorry,' he said. 'I've been very silly. I was jealous of your two humps, you see, and thought that if I ate a lot, I might grow another hump to store the surplus food. But I've only given myself a sore hump and made myself a laughing stock on the ark.'

'And I stopped eating as I was jealous of you,' said the Bactrian. 'I thought that if I stopped eating, one of my humps might disappear.'

They both turned to Mr Noah.

'Could I stay here with my friend?' asked the dromedary. 'Just until she's strong enough to walk?'

'And until *my* friend's hump has gone down, so that he can go through the doorway easily?' added the Bactrian.

They looked at one another and smiled. And Mr Noah, leaving the two camels together, made his way contentedly back towards his cabin.

7

THE SQUIRREL'S TALE

The great revolt of the animals began over a small pile of nuts taken by the squirrel. It was not as if the squirrel had *stolen* the nuts, for he had asked Ham, Mr Noah's middle son, if he could take them.

'You see my wife and I are planning to have a long sleep, which seems a sensible thing to do while we're on the ark. And when we hibernate we like to have a small stock of nuts in case we wake up and feel peckish.'

But Ham had forbidden it. 'We can't have animals hoarding food. There's only just enough to go round as it is.'

So the squirrel had gone to the food store and helped himself.

'It's not stealing,' he explained to his wife. 'For we won't be eating at all unless we wake up. We're actually doing Mr Noah a favour.'

Unfortunately Ham had not seen it that way. He had given the squirrel a telling-off, and moved the entire stock of nuts to his cabin. 'So that they'll be safe from thieves like you.'

The squirrel was very upset.

'He had no right to take my nuts away! No right at all! And I wasn't stealing. I asked him nice and politely if I could have some and what did I get in return? Rudeness!'

'Why don't you complain?' asked the peacock, fanning his beautiful tail. 'I'm always complaining. Not that anyone takes the slightest notice.'

'That's a good idea,' said the squirrel. 'I'll complain to the lion. Or the tiger. They're Mr Noah's deputies. They ought to know how I've been treated!'

'I wouldn't do that,' hissed the snake, uncoiling himself from a beam high up in the roof. 'I wouldn't go to either of them.'

'Why not?'

'Because they're on Mr Noah's side,' he hissed and coiled himself up again.

'I didn't know there were "sides",' said the racoon, who was busy washing his food.

The jackal, who had been pacing restlessly up and down the hall, stopped and stared in amazement.

'What on earth are you doing?'

The racoon looked up. 'I always wash my food before eating it. Don't you? You never know where it's been.'

'In the hands of that Ham,' said the squirrel bitterly. '*And* he's taken away the entire store of nuts so I can't get any more.'

'Typical,' said the weasel sympathetically. 'But that's

humans for you. Taking our nuts, laying down the law, not listening, it's all part and parcel of the same thing.'

'That's why we're in this pickle,' said the jackal, who had resumed pacing up and down. 'Stuck on the ark with the world flooded and no sign of the rain stopping.'

'I don't understand,' said the giraffe with a puzzled expression. 'What has the rain got to do with the squirrel's nuts?'

The jackal sighed. 'Humans have made such a mess of the world that God had to destroy it,' he said slowly. 'Do you understand that?'

The giraffe nodded his long neck.

'But when God sent the rain to flood the world, he decided to save two of every creature, so that when the rain does stop and the flood goes down we can all begin again. Got it?'

'Yes.'

'But, and this is the bit I just don't understand, God put Mr Noah in charge of the ark.'

'What's wrong with that?'

'Mr Noah is a human,' said the jackal.

The giraffe looked puzzled.

The jackal sighed. 'Why didn't God put *animals* in charge?' he asked.

'I don't know,' said the giraffe, quite pleased at being able to answer the question.

'Perhaps he never thought about it,' said the penguin. 'God can't think of everything.'

'He should have thought about it,' said the snake from his ledge high above them. 'He *is* God after all. Wiser and cleverer than all of us put together—or so we're led to believe.'

'How wise or clever was it to put Mr Noah in charge?' asked the jackal.

'I don't think Mr Noah would have taken away my nuts,' said the squirrel, after much thought.

'This,' said the jackal impatiently, 'is far more important than nuts.'

'*Nothing* is more important than nuts,' said the squirrel firmly.

'I didn't mean that it's not important...'

'I think we should support you,' said the weasel

firmly. 'This issue of the squirrel's nuts is one that should unite us all!'

'That's very true,' said the jackal. 'We must act now!'

'You'll be saying next that we should take over the ark,' the monkey said, sarcastically.

'That's exactly what we should do!'

'But I don't want to take over the ark,' protested the squirrel. My wife and I only want to hibernate with a small store of nuts in case we get hungry.'

The jackal wasn't listening.

'A committee,' he said briskly. 'We must form a committee to plan the revolt.'

'It won't work,' said the monkey drily. 'You mark my words, humans will win every time. Haven't they got God on their side?'

'Once God sees what a fine job we're making of things, he'll soon come over to our way of thinking.' He turned to the squirrel. 'You must be our leader.'

'No, really…' the squirrel protested.

'If it hadn't been for you, none of this would have started.'

'And I wish it hadn't,' the squirrel said to his wife that night.

'Don't worry,' she replied, 'it won't last. They'll soon find something else to think about. Anyway, if you're the leader you can always put a stop to it.'

But the squirrel soon found that that was easier said than done.

News of the revolt spread quickly among the animals.

Some of them agreed with it, some disagreed, but all were interested.

'We must have a simple message,' said the jackal. 'One that the less intelligent among us can understand.'

'What about "Tail good, no tail bad"?' asked the peacock, spreading out his beautiful tail.

'What's that meant to mean?' asked the guinea-pig.

'It means that you're on our side if you've got a tail and not if you haven't,' explained the peacock. 'Humans don't have tails.'

'Neither have I,' said the guinea-pig.

'Or I,' said the chimpanzee.

'And I lose my tail from time to time,' said the gecko.

The monkey grinned. 'That means you're sitting on the fence. You're not on one side or the other.'

'I think we ought to be supporting Mr Noah rather than going against him,' said the elephant. 'God's given him a hard enough job as it is.'

'Hear, hear,' said the beaver, thumping her tail on the floor.

Heated arguments continued on all sides and, from time to time, fights broke out.

Mr Noah soon realized that something was wrong. But he could not find out what it was. He asked the lion and the tiger.

'Nothing is wrong, Mr Noah,' said the lion, firmly. 'Nothing at all. I would be the first to know and I can tell you, without a shadow of a doubt, that everything is just as usual.'

The tiger nodded agreement and Mr Noah went away.

But the lion and the tiger did know about the planned revolt and had decided not to tell.

'After all,' said the tiger, 'although we are Mr Noah's deputies, he is a human and we are animals. One does have one's loyalties.'

'Yes,' agreed the lion. 'And if there had been any justice at all in the world, God would have put me in charge. I am, after all, King of the Jungle and Lord of All Beasts.'

'And big-headed too,' added the tiger sourly.

As the day of the revolt drew near, the atmosphere in the great hall grew more and more tense. Despite the assurances of the lion and the tiger, Mr Noah was convinced that something was very wrong.

'I know the animals are planning something,' he said to God 'I just wish I knew what it was. There are arguments and fights breaking out all over the place, but whenever I try to find out what's wrong, no one will tell me. Is it my fault? Have I done something wrong?'

God sighed. 'No, Noah, you have done nothing wrong. But because you are human, you are being blamed for the wickedness of the world.'

'Can I do anything to put it right?'

'You *can* put right the wrongs on the ark.'

'Tell me.'

So God told Mr Noah about the squirrel.

'I'll go and see the squirrel at once,' said Mr Noah, getting off his bed.

'No,' said God. 'Wait.'

Now while Mr Noah was talking to God, the squirrel was talking to his wife.

'I don't know what to do for the best. After all, if God had wanted to put squirrels in charge, or jackals, or weasels, he'd have done it, wouldn't he? He must have had a good reason for putting Mr Noah in charge. If only I knew what to do.'

'Perhaps you should go and see Mr Noah.'

'That's sneaking.'

'Would you like *me* to go and see Mr Noah?'

'No,' said the squirrel. 'That's not right either. Oh what shall I do? All I wanted was a small supply of nuts so we could go to sleep without worrying and now look what's happened!'

All night long he ran up and down outside his nest, worrying about what he should do. Just before morning he had come to a decision.

Head down, so that the other animals wouldn't see him, he crept along to Mr Noah's cabin and knocked on the door.

'I felt I had to tell you, Mr Noah,' he said, when he had reached the end of his story. 'Although I don't like telling tales. But it was my fault in a way that it all started, so I should be the one to try and stop it.'

'It wasn't only your fault,' Mr Noah said. 'I have already spoken to Ham, and he'll apologise and give

you some nuts so that you can go to sleep without worry. It was very brave of you to tell me. It can't have been easy.'

Mr Noah called a meeting in the great hall.

'Look,' he said, 'I'm sure that some of you would be much better at being in charge on the ark. But God gave me the job. I don't know why he did, and I didn't want to do it, but I agreed to it and now I'm trying to make the best of it for the sake of us all. So can I appeal to you to give up this idea of a revolt? If there's anything you're unhappy about, come and tell me and we'll try and work out a solution.'

The animals muttered among themselves. Then the jackal spoke.

'How did you know about the revolt?' he asked

suspiciously, glaring at the squirrel.

'God told me,' said Mr Noah.

'Oh,' said the jackal, 'well if *God* told you...'

And he slunk away to his corner of the hall. The great revolt of the animals on the ark was at an end.

8

THE CATERPILLAR'S TALE

The rain fell day after day. Inside the ark the animals, insects and birds could hear it spattering against the wooden sides and drumming on the roof. It seemed as if it would never stop.

'It's never going to end,' said the monkey. 'We'll spend the rest of our lives in this dark, leaking tub...'

'It's not leaking,' said one of the termites, who had just finished mending some holes made by the woodpeckers. 'Our work is watertight.'

'The food will run out and we'll die of hunger,' the monkey continued.

'But we have Mr Noah's promise that the rain will stop after forty days and forty nights,' the dormouse said.

'If you believe that, you'll believe anything.'

'The clouds will roll away, the sun will shine and the water will dry up.'

'Yes, and pigs might fly,' added the monkey sarcastically.

'We must have hope,' said the dormouse, 'and faith in Mr Noah.'

'I've no hope and as for faith in Mr Noah...!' The monkey turned away in disgust.

A hairy green caterpillar had been listening to this conversation as she slowly munched a tasty leaf which Shem had just provided. She looked at her friend, a white caterpillar with brown stripes.

'I didn't think pigs could fly,' she said.

'They can't,' said her friend, who was busy chewing the leaf from the other end.

The green caterpillar raised her head. 'Excuse me, pig, but can you fly?'

'Hey, is that some kind of a joke?' asked the pig. He turned to his wife. 'Honey, that caterpillar's just asked if we can fly!'

Both pigs burst out laughing.

'Told you so,' said the striped caterpillar. 'Mmm. This leaf is *good*.'

'I wish *I* could fly,' said the green caterpillar.

A bumblebee flew past her head. The caterpillar watched him.

'How do you do that?'

'What—buzz?'

'No. Fly.'

'I've got wings. That's how.'

'But I've heard,' said the caterpillar, who liked collecting bits of information, 'I've heard that bumblebees are so heavy they shouldn't be able to fly at all.'

'Are you calling me fat?'

The caterpillar looked at the bumblebee's round, striped brown and gold body.

'Oh no. Not at all. I think you're very handsome. Very handsome indeed.'

'Well then.'

'But I *have* heard that you shouldn't be able to fly.'

'Oh really?'

'Yes,' said the caterpillar earnestly. 'It's really quite impossible for you to fly.'

'No one's told me that,' said the bumblebee. He laughed and flew away.

The caterpillar watched him go. 'I do wish I could fly.'

'You're always wanting the impossible, said the striped caterpillar, starting on another leaf. 'Why can't you just be happy as you are? It's warm and it's dry and

there's a non-stop supply of leaves. A bit of sun would be nice, but you can't have everything.'

The bumblebee went into his nest. 'Do you know what I've just been told? I've been told that bumblebees can't fly!'

The other bee burst out laughing. 'No one's told *me* that!'

Both bees flew round the great hall, buzzing up and down. 'See how well we can't fly!' they shouted to the caterpillar. 'Aren't we clever!'

The caterpillar watched as she nibbled a corner of a leaf. 'There's no need to laugh. I must have got it wrong, that's all.'

The bees flew away and the caterpillar carried on eating.

'Have you ever thought how boring it is, being a caterpillar?' the caterpillar said to the bumblebee when he returned.

'I can't say I've lost any sleep over it.'

'You can fly, but I've got to walk wherever I want to go.'

'That's true, but you do have an awful lot of legs.'

'I suppose so,' sighed the caterpillar, 'but it still takes a long time to get from one end of a leaf to the other.'

'It wouldn't if you didn't stop to eat all the time.'

'But I'm always hungry.'

'That's your problem,' said the bumblebee, about to fly away.

'I've been thinking,' said the caterpillar. 'If bumblebees

can fly, even though they're not built for flying, perhaps I can fly, even though I haven't any wings.'

'Perhaps,' said the bumblebee doubtfully.

'It's worth a try anyway.'

The bumblebee watched as the caterpillar wriggled her way to the very edge of the ledge on which she was lying, bunched her legs under her and jumped…

She landed on top of the baboon.

'I didn't think it was raining caterpillars,' said the baboon, who was not very bright.

'I'm sorry,' said the caterpillar. 'I was trying to fly.'

The baboon scratched his head. 'I didn't know caterpillars could fly. Whatever next?'

The caterpillar looked at the ledge far above her and sighed. It was going to be a long, long crawl before she reached her food again.

'I could have told you that caterpillars can't fly,' said the bumblebee. 'You call *me* large, but just look at *your* funny shape! It would take a miracle to make you fly and I don't believe in miracles!'

'What's a miracle?'

'Something wonderful and amazing that doesn't normally happen.'

'Well, it's pretty wonderful and amazing that *you* can fly, seeing as you're so fat,' retorted the caterpillar crossly as she began the long crawl back.

It was late when she reached the ledge and she was tired. She nibbled part of a leaf and went to sleep. When she woke the next morning she had another idea.

'I've been thinking.'

'Again?' said the striped caterpillar through a mouthful of food. 'I wish you wouldn't. It makes my head ache.'

The caterpillar called to the bumblebee. 'I think you can fly because you have wings which you wave up and down.'

The bumblebee thought for a moment. 'That's right.'

'Well, I haven't any wings, but I do have legs. Lots of legs. If I waved them up and down, perhaps they'd do the same job as your wings and I could fly.'

'Do you really think so?'

'I don't see why not.'

'I do,' said the striped caterpillar, pausing before attacking another leaf.

But the first caterpillar was already taking a deep breath and did not listen. She closed her eyes and jumped. But this time, instead of bunching her legs under her, she waved them wildly in the air.

She landed upside down on the floor.

'Are you all right?' asked the bumblebee, flying down to join her.

'No,' said the caterpillar, trying to roll over onto her front.

'It didn't work, did it?'

'No. It didn't.'

'Told you so,' the striped caterpillar called down.

The caterpillar looked up at the ledge, high above her, and sighed at the thought of the long crawl back.

Mr Noah, walking through the great hall, only just missed stepping on her.

'Fallen off, have you?' he asked, picking her up and replacing her carefully on the ledge.

'I was trying to fly,' said the caterpillar. 'If it's a miracle that the bumblebee can fly, because he's so fat, I thought that maybe I could have a miracle too, as I do want to fly so much.'

Mr Noah smiled.

'It's a miracle we're all alive and safe on this ark when the rest of the world is flooded. Perhaps you should be content with that.'

'That's what my friend says. And it's not that I'm not grateful, but I would like a little miracle of my own. How do I make one, Mr Noah?'

'Miracles come from God. And nothing is impossible for God. You just have to hope.'

The days passed. The caterpillars ate and ate and grew to their full size, while the bees flew up and down.

'Oh, if only I could fly,' the caterpillar said, but by now she had grown so large and lazy with all the food she had eaten, she was too weary even to try. No one answered her, for the bees had gone back into their nest and the other animals in the hall were resting.

'I don't suppose I'll ever fly now,' she thought sadly and carried on eating.

A few days later the caterpillars found that they were no longer hungry, just very tired. They spun fine threads of silk around themselves until they were completely covered, then fell fast asleep.

The caterpillar woke with a start. She felt weak and cold and a bit light-headed. With some difficulty she struggled out of her cocoon and sat on the edge of the ledge. Her friend was still sleeping, snugly tucked up in her silken cocoon.

'Perhaps I overate,' thought the caterpillar. 'Or I've woken up too quickly. I think I'll just sit here quietly for a while.'

Slowly she began to feel stronger. She also felt happy. Happier than she had felt for a long, long time. She looked up, and although there was only the roof of the ark above her, and although the rain was still pouring down, the caterpillar thought that it was going to be a very fine day.

The bumblebee flew past.

'Hello, good morning!' called the caterpillar. 'What a lovely day it is!'

'Is it?'

'If I could only fly,' the caterpillar continued, 'life would be perfect, even though it's raining.'

'There's nothing to stop you,' said the bumblebee, buzzing round her head.

'Of course there is! You remember, I tried to fly but I can't. I haven't any wings.'

'Haven't any...? Is that some sort of a joke?'

'Joke?'

'You have the most beautiful wings I've ever seen,'

said the bumblebee. 'And if you can't fly with those wings, then I'm sure I can't fly with mine.'

'What do you mean?'

'Try it and you'll see!'

So the caterpillar, who was no longer a caterpillar but a beautiful butterfly, arched her back. She felt her wings begin to stir. She rose into the air and, as if she had been doing it all her life, she began to fly.

'Who said miracles don't happen?' she called to the bumblebee as she flew lightly up into the roof of the ark.

9

THE BISON'S TALE

Thud, thud, thud, thud! Mr Noah shuddered as the heavy footsteps went past his cabin.

'Left, right, left, right!' Thud! Thud…! The ark shook from side to side.

'You'll really have to do something about those bison,' said Mrs Noah the following day. 'They make such a noise and shake the ark so much, I'm sure it could capsize.'

Thud! Thud!

'Mr Noah, can't you stop those bison?' complained the ostrich. 'The noise they make has given me a dreadful headache.'

'Me too,' agreed the goat. 'And they never stop. Day and night, night and day…'

'It's bad enough being on the ark in the first place, without having two great hairy bison thundering round the place,' the peacock grumbled.

'All right,' said Mr Noah. 'I'll speak to them.'

He did not have to search very far, for they could be heard all over the ark.

Thud! Thud!

'Left, right, left, right, halt!' said the first bison. Both bison stopped.

'Mr Noah! Sir!'

They pawed the ground with their hooves.

'Two bison, present and correct...'

'...if a bit cramped,' the second bison finished.

'Not that we're complaining,' said the first bison. 'We bison were brought up to make the best of things. It's a hard life out there on the prairie.'

'We're not blaming you, Mr Noah,' said the second bison.

'Orders are orders and must be obeyed, and you've had your orders from the very top.'

'But it is a bit difficult, you must admit.'

'What is?' asked Mr Noah.

'It's just so very small.'

'Small?'

'We're used to the wide open prairies, Mr Noah,' the first bison explained. 'How I miss the great plains we used to roam across.'

'Of course, we're very grateful to be saved from the flood, and we try to make the best of it, but it is very boring roaming round and round the ark,' said the second bison.

'That's what I came to see you about,' Mr Noah said, thankful to get a word in. 'I'm afraid your roaming

has upset some of the animals.'

'Upset the animals?' said the first bison. 'Rot! Just because they won't take any exercise themselves, they shouldn't complain about those of us who like to keep fit. Do some of them good to walk around the ark a bit more.'

'Possibly,' said Mr Noah.

'Of course it would. I tell you, Mr Noah, some of those animals won't be able to walk off the ark when the flood goes down—they'll be too fat. Why, they don't even have to hunt for their food.'

'I never thought of that,' said Mr Noah, thoughtfully.

'Tell you what. We'll organize some keep-fit classes.'

The second bison nodded enthusiastically. 'That's a good idea.'

'Need a good shaking up, some of those idle good-for-nothings,' the first bison continued.

'I've had complaints about the noise you make,' said Mr Noah.

'Noise? What do you mean—noise? We just trot round the decks, that's all.'

'We can't help being rather heavy, you know,' added the second bison.

'Of course not. But could you try to trot a bit more quietly…? Not thud about, if you see what I mean…? And perhaps not *all* the time?'

'We'll do the best we can, but really, Mr Noah, we can't stop roaming.' He turned to the second bison. 'Ready?'

'Ready.'

'Forward march! Left, right, left, right…'

Mr Noah explained the situation to the rest of the animals and told them of the bison's suggestion.

'Keep-fit?' sniffed the ostrich. '*Keep-fit?* How insulting!'

The crocodile laughed so much he almost choked. 'Bison giving keep-fit lessons?'

'Say, now I've heard everything!' said the wallaby, his eyes streaming.

'What I don't like is the suggestion that we're fat and lazy,' said the pig.

'But you are,' said the crocodile. 'Very fat and very lazy.'

'That's as may be,' said the pig. 'All I said was that I don't like a loud-mouthed, heavy-footed bison telling me so.'

'I get all the exercise I need,' said the heron. 'I stand first on one leg… and then the other. It's very exhausting.'

'But is it such a bad idea?' Mr Noah looked round the assembled animals, most of whom were lying half-asleep in the great hall. 'We'll need to be fit to face all the challenges when we get off the ark.'

'Oh, I don't think you should worry too much,' said the fox. 'Show me a couple of chickens and I'll soon get fit chasing them.'

'I regard this cruise as a rest,' said the tiger, lazily flicking his tail to and fro. 'A small oasis of calm in the middle of a busy and stressful life.'

The lion snorted. 'Your life has never been busy! Everyone knows that tigers are the laziest of creatures!'

'Is that so?' asked the tiger, a dangerous glint in his eye. 'Then perhaps we should have a little warm-up exercise right now and I'll show you just how fit I am! Put your paws up!'

They circled each other, snarling.

'Tiger, lion,' said Mr Noah hurriedly. 'Please. You're my deputies and shouldn't fight.'

From then on the bison tried to walk quietly. But for some reason, the noise was a lot worse than before and the animals were soon complaining again.

'Right, left, right, left!'

Mr Noah waited for them to arrive.

'Halt!'

'I'm sorry bison, but the animals are still complaining about you.'

'You can't have a good bracing walk if you're going about on tiptoe,' said the first bison.

'We are trying to move quietly,' said the second bison.

'Perhaps if you tried moving more slowly?' Mr Noah suggested.

'Where's the exercise in that?' the first bison snapped and they set off once more.

'Did I get the measurements wrong, God?' Mr Noah asked anxiously. 'Should I have built a bigger ark?'

'No, Noah. It's just the right size. But you must realize that the ark would seem as small to large animals as it would seem large to small ones.'

Mr Noah thought about it.

'Is there anything I can do to help?'

'They will have help very soon,' God promised.

The following day the bison were stopped in the middle of their morning trot.

'Mind where you're putting your great hooves!' called a small, frightened voice at their feet.

'What's that?'

'I said, "MIND WHERE YOU'RE PUTTING YOUR GREAT FEET!" ' squeaked the ant in her loudest voice. 'YOU NEARLY SQUASHED US!'

'Terribly sorry,' said the first bison. 'I didn't see you.'

'It's very worrying, you roaming round like that. We never know when you might be coming.'

'I never thought of that.'

'We're used to roaming the wide open prairies and not used to being cramped up on a small ark,' explained the second bison.

'What do you mean, a *small* ark?' squeaked the ant. 'This place is enormous!'

'It's so enormous, we can't even imagine its size,' her husband added.

'It's tiny compared with what we're used to,' said the second bison.

The ant sighed. 'Everyone tells us that we're floating on an ark and lucky to be here and safe from the flood. But for us it's just like being on land. We've been running around, trying to see as much as we can, but even if we spent our entire lives on the ark, we'd never see more than a fraction of it.'

'And it's such an experience,' added her husband. 'One we'd love to tell the grandchildren.'

The bison looked at his wife. 'I think we've been rather selfish, don't you?'

'But it's never too late to put things right,' his wife agreed.

Soon afterwards the animals in the great hall were amazed at the sight of the two bison walking very slowly and very carefully.

'This,' the first bison was saying, 'is the great hall. It's where most of the animals, insects and birds spend their time. Am I going slowly enough for you?'

'Oh yes, thank you,' said the ant who was clinging to his back.

They walked out.

'Well I never,' said the mandrill, scratching his pink and red bottom.

'You could knock me down with a baboon,' agreed the wallaby.

'This,' the second bison was explaining, 'is the lower

deck. And here are the great doors which God himself closed when all of us were safely inside.'

'Can we stop for a moment? It's all so big, it's a bit hard to take it in.'

'Of course. Take as much time as you like.'

Both bison stopped and waited patiently.

'It's really very kind of you to give us this guided tour,' said the ant shyly. 'You must have far more important things to do.'

'We're enjoying it,' said the bison. 'It's made me look at the ark in quite a different way. I'll never complain of it being too small again.'

Mr Noah, on his way to the great hall, smiled to see the bison and the ants.

'Thank you, God,' he said. 'I knew you would sort things out.'

'I care for the small as well as the large, Noah,' God replied.

Inside the hall the animals were quiet and rather thoughtful.

'Say, Mr Noah,' said the wallaby. 'I've been thinking. Perhaps this keep-fit thing isn't such a bad idea after all. Would you speak to the bison about it?'

'Of course,' said Mr Noah.

10
THE FLEA'S TALE

When God told Mr Noah that he was going to flood the world but that two of every animal, insect and bird should be taken onto the ark to be saved, the two fleas nearly got left behind. It was only when Mr Noah caught sight of the chimpanzees scratching themselves that he thought about the fleas and asked God whether or not they should be saved from the flood.

'Two of *every* creature must be saved,' God said.

Mr Noah scratched his head. 'If you say so, God. But the animals won't like it.'

The animals did not like it, not only because the fleas made them itch. From the moment they boarded the ark—on the backs of the two monkeys—the fleas annoyed the animals.

'I say, I say, I say, have you heard the one about the dog that visited the flea-circus and stole the show?' one of them said, jumping onto the dog's back.

The dog sighed.

The other flea joined him.

'Why did the fly fly?'

'I don't know,' said the first flea. 'Why did the fly fly?'

'Because the spider spied her!'

'I don't wish to know that. Kindly leave the dog.' Both fleas rocked with laughter.

'If you must tell jokes, would you mind not doing it on my back?' asked the dog patiently.

'Whoops, there we go again,' said the first flea. 'Upsetting the natives!'

'Where shall we go now?' asked the second flea.

'How about... the horse? He looks as if he needs cheering up.'

'Why couldn't the pony talk?'

'I don't know the answer to that one. Why couldn't the pony talk?'

'Because he was a little horse! A little hoarse. Get it?'

The fleas laughed even more.

'Now watch this, everyone!' the first flea called in a loud voice. 'My friend and I will perform our latest, death-defying leap from the back of the dog, right across the great hall, and onto the back of the horse.'

'Must you?' asked the horse.

'We will do this,' continued the first flea, 'in one mighty spring, with two back somersaults and a forward flip! Never, in the entire history of the ark, has anything so daring been attempted before!'

'That's not much of a claim, as the ark's brand new,'

said the mongoose. 'But I don't mind what you do, so long as you don't land on me.'

'Allez-oup!' called the fleas and the mongoose began to scratch herself.

'I think you don't entirely understand,' said the first flea, 'just how lucky you are to have my friend and me. We're not your average common-or-garden fleas. Oh no. We are Fleance and Fleaty, your world-famous performing fleas. We come from a long, long line of theatrical fleas...'

'...whose ancestors had Adam and Eve roaring with laughter in the Garden of Eden,' added the second flea.

'...now alas the sole surviving members.'

'Don't count your chickens before they're hatched,' advised the fox. 'You might not survive very long.'

'Why did the fox cross the road?' asked Fleance.

'Because he saw a couple of chickens!' The fleas laughed.

'My turn now,' said Fleaty. 'On which side do chickens have the most feathers?'

'I don't know, Fleaty, on which side do chickens have the most feathers?'

'On the outside of course!'

Both fleas laughed so much they had to clutch tightly onto the mongoose to prevent themselves from falling off.

'We don't care for jokes about us,' said one of the chickens.

'We don't care for your jokes at all,' said the fox.

'But we're here to entertain you,' said Fleance. 'We'll perform amazing acrobatic feats on and off the backs of your good selves. Just watch this…!'

'What?' asked the donkey.

'Ouch!' said the yak, beginning to scratch himself.

'Didn't you see how we somersaulted off the back of the mongoose, did a triple turn in the air and landed on the yak's back?'

'How many yaks does it take to…' Fleance began.

'Oh get off my back!' said the yak crossly.

'I didn't see anything,' said the donkey.

'That's because you weren't watching,' said Fleaty. 'Let me ask you a question.'

'I'm not very clever with questions,' said the donkey cautiously.

'You'll get this one. Now listen carefully.'

The donkey pricked back his ears.

'Is it raining *outside*?'

The donkey looked pleased. 'I know the answer to that,' he said proudly. 'Yes. It is raining outside.'

'Does it ever rain *inside*?' said Fleaty and both fleas burst out laughing.

The donkey looked puzzled. 'I don't think I quite understand…' he began.

'Ask you another. When do you see cows with eight feet?'

The donkey shook his head. 'I don't know.'

'When two cows are side by side!'

'Is this sort of vulgar humour going to continue for the entire voyage?' asked the emu.

'Probably,' said Fleance.

'In that case, I shall definitely complain to Mr Noah!'

'Is he "The Management?" ' asked Fleance.

'Yes,' said the emu.

'Under God,' the dormouse added. 'God's really in charge.'

'Time to move on,' said Fleance. 'Now watch this, everyone!'

The animals watched, but it was only when the

jaguar began to scratch that they realized that the fleas had jumped.

'I didn't see anything,' said the donkey.

'Then you missed the performance of a lifetime,' said Fleance sadly. 'I think I surpassed myself there. I've never managed a triple somersault at the same time as a triple back-flip. I don't suppose I'll ever do it again.'

'Well I think it's a load of nonsense,' snapped the jaguar.

'No it's not. It's a triple somersault at the same time as a triple back-flip.'

'Rubbish! It's an illusion!'

'I thought it was Fleance the flea, not an illusion,' said the donkey. 'What is an illusion? Is it another animal?'

'An illusion is when you're tricked into thinking you've seen something that didn't happen,' said the eagle swooping down from his usual perch high up in the rafters.

The donkey shook his head. 'I don't understand.'

'I'm not surprised,' said Fleance.

'I feel a headache coming on,' complained the ostrich.

'To put it another way,' said the lion grandly, '—and as King of the Jungle, I know about these things—it's when you believe in something that you can't see and doesn't exist.'

'But if you can't see it and it doesn't exist, why should you believe in it?' asked the llama.

'Why indeed?' said the lion, who had no idea of the answer but didn't want anyone else to know.

'You mean, like God?' asked the donkey, after much thought.

'No,' said the eagle. 'Not like God. You can't see God but he does exist so he's not an illusion.'

'Which brings us back to my triple somersault and triple back-flip,' said Fleance brightly.

'If you pesky fleas don't stop squirming around and making me scratch, I'm going to get very angry indeed!' said the jaguar crossly.

'Do you know what animal eats the least?' asked Fleance.

'No, what animal eats the least?' Fleaty replied.

'A moth. It just eats holes!'

Mr Noah soon found himself surrounded by angry animals, insects and birds.

'It's very wearing, having to listen to all those jokes,' said the goose.

'They're such bad jokes as well,' said the mongoose.

'Do you think so?' asked the donkey. 'I think they're rather good myself. At least, I don't really understand them, but I'm sure they're very funny.'

'They give me a headache,' said the ostrich.

'And those fleas jump from one animal to another without so much as a "Do you mind?" or "Will it trouble you if I sit on your back for a while?",' said the yak. 'It's very rude of them.'

'They make me itch,' said the rat.

'All right, all right!' said Mr Noah. 'I'll go and talk to them.'

But the fleas, seeing Mr Noah approach, decided to play hide-and-seek with him. After an hour spent running all over the ark, Mr Noah was very cross and quite worn out.

'I'll have to speak to God about you two,' he said. 'So I hope you're listening, wherever you are.'

'We're here,' said Fleance.

Mr Noah scratched his hand. 'Where?'

'On your hand,' said Fleaty.

'This behaviour has got to stop,' said Mr Noah severely. The fleas sighed.

'It's very sad,' said Fleance. 'We only want to be friends.'

'That's why we keep hopping from one animal to another,' said Fleaty. 'Just hoping that someone will like us enough to let us stay with them.'

'You must stop annoying the animals.'

'All right,' said Fleance.

'If you say so,' agreed Fleaty.

Two days later Mr Noah was visited by Mrs Noah.

'Mr Noah, you must do something about those fleas,' said Mrs Noah.

'What have they done now?'

'If they're not jumping on to me, they're jumping onto Rachel and Miriam. We've all been scratching. You must speak to God.'

So Mr Noah spoke to God.

'There doesn't seem to be an answer, God. I really don't know what to do about them.'

'There's always an answer.'

'I can only think of drowning them.'

'You'd have to catch them first,' God said, with a smile in his voice.

'It's no laughing matter!' Mr Noah said severely.

'I'm sorry, Noah, but think of it from the fleas' point of view. They want to be accepted, they want to be friends, yet everyone rejects them.'

There was a knock on the door of the cabin. It was the two hedgehogs.

'Excuse us, Mr Noah, if we're interrupting anything, but we've a suggestion to make about the fleas.'

'Come in. Any suggestion would be most welcome.'

'The thing is, we're used to providing homes for fleas. We've got thick skins and don't mind them...'

'So long as they behave themselves,' added the other hedgehog.

'We don't even mind their jokes, so long as they tell them to each other and don't bother us with them.'

Mr Noah got to his feet.

'You're an answer to a prayer,' he said simply.

So the fleas found a home on the backs of the hedgehogs and, by agreement, limited their jokes to three a day. And the fleas performed feats of daring at the party organized by the elephants and everyone applauded, although no one could actually see their amazing acrobatic moves—not even the donkey who tried very hard.

'It must have been that thing they called an illusion,' he told his wife later that night. 'But a very clever one. It had all of us fooled.'

His wife looked at him with affection. 'I expect you're right,' she said gently.

11
THE SPARROW'S TALE

After forty days and forty nights of rain, a great wind began to blow, sending the clouds scudding this way and that across the sky. The eagle was the first to bring the news to the ark, flying in through the trapdoor in the roof and crying in his loudest voice, 'The rain has stopped!'

Mr Noah poked his head out into the air and felt the fresh wind on his face. The animals and insects all cheered while the birds streamed out of the ark and soared into the air. There were larks and linnets, swallows and chaffinches, owls, blackbirds, thrushes, wrens and many, many more besides. All the birds of God's creation rose into the air and flew round and round, swooping and diving, singing, warbling, glad to feel the wind under their wings once more.

Everyone was happy that day, except for Hannah, wife of Mr Noah's youngest son Japheth. This was strange, for during the forty days and forty nights of rain when everyone on the ark had, at times, felt sad,

Hannah had always remained happy and smiling. She had a smile for everyone, and she was always singing, whether she was taking food to the animals, cleaning their quarters or tending those who were hurt. She was kind and she was gentle.

'Hannah is the sunshine on the ark,' Mr Noah had said to his wife many times.

But on the day the rain finally stopped Hannah, after opening the trapdoor in the roof and looking out on the world for the first time, burst into tears.

'Whatever is the matter?' Japheth asked anxiously.

Hannah shook her head.

'Hannah, what's wrong?' asked Mr Noah.

'I never realized it before,' she sobbed.

'Realized what?'

'I never really believed that the whole world would be flooded.'

Mr Noah was silent.

'You see, I thought that when the rain stopped, we'd all go back to the farm and that the lovely garden I made would still be there, filled with flowers and birds. I never really thought that we would never go back.'

'I see,' said Mr Noah sadly. 'I'm very sorry.'

So while the sun grew daily stronger in the sky and the flood waters slowly subsided, Hannah stayed in her cabin. She grew pale and thin and everyone worried about her.

'When we find land, we will plant a new garden,' Mr Noah promised.

'It won't be the same,' Hannah said.

'No. But with God's help it will be as beautiful.'

The animals, insects and birds all tried to help, for everyone loved Hannah. The cow gave her fresh milk, the giraffe told her a long and not very funny story, the spiders spun her a gossamer scarf, the peacock gave her one of his precious tail feathers. Even the lion and the tiger paid her a visit. And as for the birds! They flew in and out of her cabin singing all her favourite songs, but Hannah grew weaker day by day.

It was some time before the sparrow heard about Hannah. Small and brown and timid, he was scared of the other birds on the ark. He tried to keep out of their way, for they had not been kind to him.

'How dare you!' the hawk had said when the sparrow had taken a small crumb from the bird table. 'Just who do you think you are to take the last, the best, the choicest crumb?'

'Only a sparrow,' said the sparrow humbly.

'A sparrow,' said the hawk. 'An ordinary sparrow.'

'Very ordinary,' said the peacock, looking down his long nose. 'Not beautiful like me.'

'No. I'm not beautiful.'

'And not accomplished either,' said the nightingale. 'I don't suppose for a moment that you can sing.'

'I *can* sing, but not as well as you.'

'Are you wise?' asked the owl, blinking rapidly. 'I am. I can tell you the exact position of the ark in relation to the sun.'

'A fat lot of use that is,' retorted the hawk. He looked at the sparrow. 'You're common,' he said. 'The most common of all the wild birds. In fact you're so common, I wouldn't even bother to eat you unless I was absolutely starving.'

The sparrow had flown away to a dark corner of the ark high up in the roof.

'The other birds called me common,' he said to his wife.

'They don't really mean it,' she replied.

'They said I was ordinary, not beautiful like the peacock.'

'Who would want to be like that stuck-up bird?'

'I'm not wise like the owl.'

'I think you're very clever.'

'But what they said was true,' said the sparrow. 'I am small and brown and ordinary and it makes me very sad.'

'Take no notice,' said his wife, but the sparrow grew more and more unhappy. He stopped eating and would have died if Hannah had not seen him one day, sitting hunched up in a dark corner. She had taken him in her hands, stroked his wings and spoken to him kindly. She fed him herself until he was strong. So when he heard how sick Hannah was, he flew into her cabin early one morning, perched on her pillow and gazed sadly at her pale, thin face.

'Is there anything I can do to help?' he asked. 'I can't sing like the nightingale, and I haven't any beautiful tail feathers to give you like the peacock. I'm not clever like the owl, but if there is anything, please tell me.'

Hannah turned to watch him. 'A leaf from a tree in my garden,' she said in a faint voice. 'So I'd know it hadn't all been destroyed.'

'But that's impossible.'

'That's all I want.'

The sparrow went away sadly.

'Are you all right?' Mr Noah asked, seeing him flying past. The sparrow told him and Mr Noah shook his head.

'I have no idea where in the world we are. We could be miles and miles from Hannah's garden. And even if we are floating above it, there would be nothing left

106

now.' He looked at the sparrow. 'Besides, you're not strong enough to go on such a journey and anyway it isn't necessary. The dove has gone looking for land. Why don't you go back to Hannah and sing to her instead? I know she likes your company.'

The sparrow thanked Mr Noah for his advice and flew away.

'I did do right, didn't I God?' Mr Noah asked, once the sparrow had gone.

'You did what you thought best,' God replied.

The sparrow, meanwhile, had gone back to his nest, eaten a large meal, kissed his wife and flown out of the trapdoor in the roof. He had a task to perform. All that day he flew over the sea, his small bright eyes looking for signs of land. He flew towards the sun and when the sun sank and it grew dark, he flew by the light of the full moon.

He was hungry and thirsty and his wings felt so tired it became an effort to keep himself up in the air. As the sun rose the following morning, the sparrow could scarcely fly. His throat was dry, his eyes kept misting over and his wings hurt every time he flapped them feebly up and down.

'Mr Noah was right,' he thought. 'I'm not strong enough.'

And on that thought his wings failed him and he began to fall.

But instead of plunging into the cold sea, his fall was broken by one single branch, sticking out from above the water. On it was a handful of leaves.

The sparrow weakly plucked at one and it came away in his beak.

'It's too late,' he thought sadly. 'I'll never have the strength to fly back to the ark.' And he closed his eyes as he felt himself slipping from the branch.

But at that moment a wind arose. The sparrow's feathers began to ruffle. Feebly he flapped, once, twice. The wind caught under his wings, bore him up from the branch and took him high over the sea.

Inside the ark Mr Noah was talking to God about the missing sparrow.

'I'm so worried about him, for he's very small.'

'He has a big heart,' God said.

'I know, but he's not strong. I'm afraid he might have drowned.'

While Mr Noah was talking to God, the wind died down and the sparrow, still with the leaf held tightly in his beak, fell in through the trapdoor in the roof and onto the floor of the ark. No one saw him arrive. With his last ounce of strength he made his way to Hannah's cabin and laid the leaf on the pillow beside her bed.

Hannah looked at it with wondering eyes. She touched it gently. Then she looked at the sparrow and saw how thin and tired he was.

'You fetched that, for me?'

'Yes.'

'From a tree from my garden?'

The sparrow sighed. 'I don't know. It might have been.'

Slowly she sat up in bed and picked up the sparrow gently in her hands.

'I'm sure it was.' She smiled at the sparrow and stroked his small head. 'Thank you. Thank you so very much. Now we must find some food and water for you and then we'll look for land and a place where I can plant a new garden. Will you come and live there?'

'Oh yes. Please,' said the sparrow.

A short time later Mr Noah knocked on the door of Hannah's cabin and was surprised to find it empty.

'You'll find Hannah and the sparrow on the roof,' God told him.

Mr Noah picked up the single green leaf, still lying on Hannah's pillow, and stared at it in amazement.

'Don't ask,' said God, gently.

12

THE DOLPHIN'S TALE

The ark, which God had told Mr Noah to build in order to save his family and two of every animal, insect and bird from the flood, drifted on the wide open sea. The rain had stopped and a bright sun shone from a cloudless sky. The animals, pleased to get into the fresh air, took turns to sit on the roof, laze in the sun and search for land.

'Although I don't know how we head for land even if we find it,' said the monkey, 'considering that the ark can't be steered.'

The beaver shook his head. 'Pity there are no oars on board,' he said. 'Big mistake.'

'We'll just have to wait until the flood has gone down,' said the tiger. 'I don't mind.' He stretched himself lazily. 'This is the life. I could get quite used to sea cruises.'

'Speak for yourself,' said one of the reindeer. 'It's a bit too warm for me.'

'We'll see land soon,' said the dove in her gentle voice. 'It's some days since I found the olive branch, and the heat of the sun must be drying up the flood waters.'

The eagle, who was flying high above them, looked at the empty seas around the ark, sighed and shook his head.

'It's very sad to think that we are the only creatures left alive.'

But the eagle was wrong. There were plenty of other creatures still alive in the world, for the seas were teeming with fish, and when the ark first began to float, they swam around it with interest.

'Funny old vessel, when all's said and done,' sniffed a shark.

'Not like anything I've ever seen,' said a flounder. He dived underneath. 'I'm surprised it floats,' he said,

when he had finished his inspection.

'Do you see all those animals?' asked a sardine.

'There'll be rich pickings when it sinks,' the shark grinned, showing razor-sharp teeth. The smaller fish swam hurriedly away.

'Do you think it'll sink?' asked a whale.

'Bound to.'

'Well I've never seen anything like it,' said a dolphin. 'What do you think it is?'

'A flash in the pan,' said an electric eel.

'Come away, children! You might get hurt,' said a large porpoise, guiding a school of smaller porpoises well out of range.

As the days passed and the ark did not sink, most of the fish lost interest and swam off. But the dolphin stayed, wondering what such a strange vessel was doing there.

'Where do you think it's going?' she asked a sea urchin.

'Search me.'

'It's very peculiar. There's no sail and no one's rowing.'

And as the rain fell and water covered the earth, the dolphin remained with the ark.

'I'd love to be on that boat,' she said to a passing halibut.

'Well I wouldn't,' the halibut replied. 'Not with all those fish-eating animals on board. You mark my words,' he continued, severely. 'No good ever came of mixing with animals.'

But the dolphin wasn't listening and the halibut swam away.

For forty days and forty nights, while the world was covered with grey skies and driving rain, the dolphin swam beside the ark. When the rain stopped and the sun came out, the birds streamed out into the brilliant blue sky and the animals and insects crowded onto the roof. The dolphin swam closer and wished and wished she could join them until at last she could bear it no longer. She waited for a big wave and, as it bore her upwards, she leaped high into the air.

She landed on the deck, right on top of the tiger.

'Oouf!' said the tiger. 'What hit me?'

'Is God throwing thunderbolts?' asked the lizard.

'I'm sorry,' said the dolphin. 'I didn't mean to squash you.'

'Hello,' said Mr Noah. 'Where have you sprung from?'

'The sea.'

A group of interested animals had gathered by this time and were circling the dolphin warily.

'Just look at that!' said the donkey, in amazement. 'This voyage has been full of surprises. No sooner have I met all the wonderful animals, insects and birds on the ark, than a fish drops in!'

'I'm not a fish,' said the dolphin. 'I'm a mammal.'

'You're a stowaway,' said the goose in a sharp voice, 'and you shouldn't be on this ark at all!' She stretched her long neck and began to hiss.

'You mustn't do that,' said Mr Noah. 'The dolphin is our guest.'

'Uninvited,' said the mongoose.

'Have you paid your passage?' demanded the aardvark.

'No.'

'Neither have you,' the lizard retorted to the aardvark, 'so pipe down.'

'We're God's chosen,' said the goose, self-righteously. 'God didn't choose you, so I think you should leave.'

'I'm sorry, but I'm not sure I can.'

'What made you come aboard in the first place?' asked Mr Noah. 'Was it an accident?'

'Well, no,' said the dolphin. 'Not really. I've followed you the whole of the voyage. It's been very boring since the world was flooded, for there haven't been any bays for me to explore and I like doing that.' She sighed.

'It looked such fun on the ark.'

'Fun!' said the monkey sourly. 'That's the last thing I'd call it.'

'I think it's very nice to meet a dolphin,' said the elephant. 'Not the kind of creature one gets to meet in the normal course of things. I'm pleased to make your acquaintance.'

The dolphin was a source of great interest to the animals, insects and birds on the ark and a steady stream of them visited her. But as the day wore on and the hot sun beat down on the dolphin's back, she began to get tired.

'It's been very nice meeting you all, but I think I'd like to go home now,' she said at last in a faint voice. 'I'm not feeling at all well.'

Mr Noah touched her. Her skin felt dry and rough.

'Water,' she said in a thread of a voice. 'I need water. My skin mustn't dry out.'

'I'll see what I can do.'

Mr Noah went to his cabin to talk to God.

'Speak to the elephants,' God said. 'They'll help.'

So Mr Noah spoke to the elephants.

'Leave it to us,' they said and leaned over the side of the ark. They drew water up into their long trunks then turned and sprayed it over the dolphin. The dolphin began to revive.

'I've been very silly,' she told Mr Noah. 'If I was in the sea now, I'd be riding on the waves and playing with the other dolphins. Why did I ever think it would

be more fun on the ark?' She gazed longingly at the sea. 'I wish I could go back.'

Mr Noah again talked with God.

'How can I return her to the sea, God? She's so heavy and slippery as well. I'm afraid of hurting her. But I don't think she'll survive for long on the ark.'

'No,' said God. 'She must go back. Why not talk to the largest animals on the ark? They might help.'

So Mr Noah called a meeting of the biggest and heaviest animals on the ark. The rhinoceros, the hippopotamus, the bison, the oxen and all the other large animals joined the elephants beside the dolphin.

'What's this all about?' asked the rhinoceros.

But no one answered, for the ark was beginning to tilt under the weight of the heavy animals crowded to one side. And as more heavy animals came, the ark tilted further. Slowly the dolphin began to move. Faster and faster she slid towards the edge of the deck until, with a splash that caused a wave of water to soak all the large animals, the dolphin slid into the sea.

'Quickly!' Mr Noah called to the heaviest animals. 'Half of you hurry to the other side of the ark, or we'll capsize!'

And with a noise like thunder, the bison and the rhinoceros stampeded round to the other side and the ark righted itself.

'I feel seasick,' groaned the emu.

'Thank you!' called the dolphin, ducking and diving. 'Thank you, Mr Noah! Thank you, elephants and animals! Is there anything I can do in return?'

'If you see land, come and tell us!' Mr Noah called back, and the dolphin raced away.

'So that's that little excitement over,' said the tiger, resuming his perch on top of the roof the following day.

'It was very upsetting,' said the emu. 'I was sure we were going to capsize.'

'But it made a change,' said the aardvark. 'Added a bit of fun to an otherwise dull and boring life.' He looked out to sea. 'No sign of land.'

'No sign of anything,' said the goose.

'But land can't be far away,' insisted the dove in her

gentle voice. 'I did find a leaf and a twig, remember.'

The emu sniffed. '*And* you've never let us forget it.'

'You're only jealous because you didn't find it,' said the aardvark.

There was a sudden commotion on deck. The dolphin had returned and was swimming up and down.

'Land!' she called. 'Tell Mr Noah I've found land!'

Mr Noah came running. 'Where? Is it far?'

'Not far,' said the dolphin, turning and swimming off. 'Follow me!'

'We can't! We can't steer the ark.'

The beaver shook his head. 'What did I say?' he asked of no one in particular. 'Big mistake not having oars.'

The dolphin swam back. 'Can't steer the ark?'

'No,' said Mr Noah. 'We've no sail and no oars.'

The dolphin swam off.

'I know that there must have been a good reason for not bringing a sail or oars,' said Mr Noah that night as he sat in his cabin and talked to God. 'Otherwise you would have told me to take them. So please don't think I'm doubting you, for you've brought us all this way in safety. But it is a bit hard to know that land is so near and we can't get to it.'

'Now Noah,' said God, 'have a little more faith.'

'Yes,' said Noah. 'I'll try.'

Early the following morning, when Mr Noah was on the roof of the ark watching the sun come up and flood the world, he saw a disturbance in the water. It looked at first like huge waves, but as it grew lighter, Mr Noah could see that the waves were caused by shoals and shoals of fish who were following the dolphin.

'We've come to guide you to land,' called the dolphin. 'Now then everyone, surround the ark!'

Four dolphins, two sharks, a killer whale and a whole school of porpoises surrounded the ark.

'All right?' called the dolphin. 'Now SWIM!'

And together the fish began swimming, with the ark in their midst.

'Thank you!' Mr Noah shouted.

'Thank you, thank you!' shouted the animals and insects, while the birds flew high up into the air.

Swiftly the ark was carried along and soon Mr Noah could see land.

'The current will take you, now,' said the dolphin. 'Goodbye, Mr Noah. Goodbye elephants. Thank you for saving my life. Goodbye animals. It's been fun meeting you all.'

With a last wave of her fin, she and all the fish veered off and swam away.

'Thank you, God,' said Mr Noah as the ark finally began to head towards land.

13
THE RAINBOW'S END

The ark came to rest with a bump on the top of a mountain called Ararat.

'We've landed!' called the giraffe, who was up on the roof at the time. In his excitement, he tumbled down the steps and fell into the great hall.

'Are you sure?' asked the panther.

'Ouch!' said the giraffe, rubbing his long neck. 'Of course I'm sure!'

'Hooray!' shouted the elephant, lifting up her trunk.

'At last!' exclaimed the cheetah. 'A really good, fast run in the fresh air!'

'A gallop across the wide open prairies!' the bison shouted.

'A wallow in a first-rate watering-hole!' thundered the rhinoceros.

'A stream or two to dam,' said the beaver in a quieter, more uncertain voice.

The animals looked at one another, then fell silent.

'And yet...' the beaver began.

'Exactly,' said the cheetah.

'Just what I was thinking,' said the elephant.

'What do you think it's like out there?' asked the ostrich. 'Is it—well—safe?'

'Being on the ark might have its drawbacks, but at least it's safe,' said the emu thoughtfully.

The tiger looked at her in astonishment. 'I thought you hated it here. You've moaned about it often enough.'

'Well, I know,' the emu agreed. 'But that's just me—always moaning. You shouldn't have taken any notice.'

'We didn't,' said the tiger.

'Quiet!' called the eagle. 'The great moment has arrived!'

'I should have said that,' complained the lion. 'After all, I am Mr Noah's deputy.'

'*One* of Mr Noah's deputies,' added the tiger.

Mr Noah, his wife, his three sons and their wives entered the big hall.

'Strange that,' said the fox. 'Something I've never thought of before.'

'What?' buzzed one of the wasps.

'Why do you think God allowed Mr Noah to bring his entire family on the ark? After all, there's only two of each of us.'

'Favouritism,' said the monkey sourly. 'God likes humans better than he likes us.'

'Oh, I don't think so,' said the beaver. 'I think we've all been very privileged and shouldn't complain.'

'Hear, hear,' said the emu, and everyone turned to stare at her in astonishment.

'Eight,' said the owl suddenly.

'Eight what?' asked the beaver.

'Eight humans. Mr Noah, Mrs Noah—that makes two. Their sons, Shem, Ham and Japheth—that's three more, making…' he thought for a moment, 'five. And their three wives—that makes eight.'

'Wonderful!' said the monkey sarcastically.

'It is, isn't it,' said the donkey sincerely. 'I couldn't do sums like that in my head.'

'I am rather good at sums,' said the owl, blinking his eyelids rapidly.

'I think God let Mr Noah bring all his family because there was far too much work just for two of them,' the dormouse said thoughtfully. 'Looking after us can't have been easy.'

'If it hadn't been for Mr Noah, we would never have been saved from the flood,' added the beaver.

'If it hadn't been for humans, God wouldn't have had to flood the world in the first place,' muttered the jackal quietly, but no one was listening, for at that moment Mr Noah opened the great doors of the ark.

Sunlight streamed in. The animals made a rush for the exit.

'Line up there!' snarled the tiger, suddenly remembering his position as one of Mr Noah's deputies. 'Two by two, that's right. No pushing or shoving. Let's show God that we know how to behave.'

The animals lined up and Mr Noah led them off the ark and onto dry land.

'It feels… kinda funny,' said the pig, trotting uncertainly on the thick green grass. 'Don't you feel it should be rolling from side to side?'

'Oh, how good to stretch my legs!' said the bison. He looked down at the ants, scurrying beside him. 'Can we give you a lift anywhere?'

The ants stopped scurrying. 'No,' said one of them

uncertainly, 'for I don't know where we're going.'

And indeed all the animals and insects were stopping, looking round them almost fearfully.

'It's just a bit… well, frightening to start again,' said the mole. 'We could start digging, I suppose, but somehow…' her voice trailed off.

Even the birds had alighted on the ground, as if afraid to fly away.

'It's all so… so *big*,' said the bison. 'Silly, really, when I've been complaining about the ark being so small.'

'We've grown used to being on the ark,' said the leopard.

'*Too* used to it,' said the rat drily. 'Like prisoners being scared when they're given their freedom.'

'And *you'd* know all about prisons,' said the peacock. He unfurled his bright tail then shivered. 'The wind feels strange on my tail,' he said and closed it with a snap.

Everyone fell silent and turned to Mr Noah, and Mr Noah, who had spent the morning preparing a long farewell speech, looked at the animals, insects and birds and forgot every single word. He felt just as anxious as they did.

'I could almost wish we were still on board the ark,' he thought.

Suddenly a cloud passed in front of the sun. The fox looked up.

'Don't look now, but I think it's going to rain,' he said. 'Here we go again, everyone back on the ark!' There was even a note of relief in his voice.

The animals began to move towards the ark as the first drops of rain fell.

'Is it true, Mr Noah?' bleated the goat. 'Is the flood starting again?'

'Hey, wait a minute,' said the pig, stopping suddenly. 'I thought we'd gotten through most of the food. How are we going to survive?'

The animals stopped and stared at Mr Noah.

'Is it all starting again, God?' Mr Noah asked.

'Look up, Noah,' said God.

Mr Noah looked up. Although it was still raining, the sun had come out from behind the cloud. Clear against the sky, Mr Noah could see a shimmering light. Red, orange, yellow, green, blue, indigo and violet, the glowing rainbow formed an archway which stretched across the sky.

'This rainbow is a sign of my promise to you,' God said. 'Never again will I send a flood to destroy the earth. Whenever you see a rainbow in the sky, you will be reminded of this promise. Now speak to the animals, Noah. Give them hope for the future and strength to meet the challenges that lie ahead.'

'But I'm frightened, too, God,' said Mr Noah. 'And I've forgotten the speech I'd prepared.'

'Just speak from your heart,' said God. 'And leave the rest to me.'

So, for the last time, Mr Noah stepped forward and held up his hand. The animals fell silent.

'Animals,' Mr Noah said in a loud voice. 'Insects and

birds. My friends. I've only ever tried to do what God wanted, and sometimes I didn't do very well. But it's God who's really been in charge and always will be. Just trust in God and you'll be all right.'

'Will we ever see you again?' asked the dormouse.

'You know where to find me,' said Mr Noah. 'You're welcome at any time.' He looked at the fleas. '*All* of you.'

With that he held up his hands and blessed them, then called goodbye as the animals went their separate ways.

'So now it's all over, God,' Mr Noah said, a little sadly, when the last animal had gone.

'No, Noah,' said God. 'Look around you. It's a new beginning.'

As Mr Noah looked around him, the rain stopped, the clouds rolled away and the sun shone in a brilliant blue sky. Raindrops glittered and sparkled like gems on the fresh green grass and hung dripping from the leaves of the trees.

And as Mr Noah stared closer at the round droplets of water, he suddenly caught his breath. For there, reflected deep in the heart of each tiny drop of rain, was the image of a rainbow.

'Thank you, God,' said Mr Noah contentedly. 'It's good to be home.'